SELECTED SECULAR
AND SACRED SONGS

RECENT RESEARCHES IN AMERICAN MUSIC

H. Wiley Hitchcock, general editor

A-R Editions, Inc., publishes six quarterly series—

Recent Researches in the Music of the Middle Ages and Early Renaissance
Margaret Bent, general editor

Recent Researches in the Music of the Renaissance
James Haar, general editor

Recent Researches in the Music of the Baroque Era
Robert L. Marshall, general editor

Recent Researches in the Music of the Classical Era
Eugene K. Wolf, general editor

Recent Researches in the Music of the Nineteenth and Early Twentieth Centuries
Rufus Hallmark, general editor

Recent Researches in American Music
H. Wiley Hitchcock, general editor—

which make public music that is being brought to light
in the course of current musicological research.

Each volume in the *Recent Researches* is devoted
to works by a single composer or to a single genre of composition,
chosen because of its potential interest to scholars and performers,
and prepared for publication according to the standards that govern
the making of all reliable historical editions.

Correspondence should be addressed:

A-R EDITIONS, INC.
315 West Gorham Street
Madison, Wisconsin 53703

RECENT RESEARCHES IN AMERICAN MUSIC • VOLUME XV

Benjamin Carr

SELECTED SECULAR AND SACRED SONGS

Edited by Eve R. Meyer

A-R EDITIONS, INC. • MADISON

Library of Congress Cataloging in Publication Data

Carr, Benjamin, 1768–1831.
   [Songs.   Selections]
   Selected secular and sacred songs.

   (Recent researches in American music, ISSN 0147–0078 ; v. 15)
   Bibliography: p.
   1. Songs with piano.   I. Meyer, Eve R.   II. Series.
M2.3.U6R4   vol. 15   [M1620]   85–750122
ISBN 0–89579–204–4

Contents

Preface

The Composer

From the time of his arrival in Philadelphia in 1793 until his death in 1831, Benjamin Carr was in the forefront of musical life in America. Being an energetic man with diverse talents, he successfully pursued a multifaceted career as composer,[1] performer, teacher, conductor, church musician, concert manager, publisher, editor, and music dealer.

The Carr family had been associated with music and the music trade for several generations in London, dating back to John Carr (fl. 1672–95), who opened a publishing house and music store at Middle Temple Gate about 1672. Continuing in the family tradition, Joseph Carr (1739–1819), Benjamin's father, operated a musical repository at Middle Row, Holborn, and introduced his sons into the business. Benjamin Carr is known to have opened his own London musical repository in Old Round Court Strand possibly as early as 1786.[2] Little additional information is available on Benjamin Carr's early life, except that he was born on 12 September 1768 and studied with his father, who was an organist. Carr also studied with such distinguished musicians as Samuel Arnold, composer of operas and sacred music and organist at Westminster Abbey, and with Charles Wesley, organist, harpsichordist, and composer.[3] By his early twenties, Carr's career as a performer and composer was well established. He was principal tenor and harpsichordist at the Academy of Ancient Music, and he occasionally served as conductor there.[4] His most significant London composition was his first opera, *Philander and Silvia, or Love Crowned at Last*, which was performed at Sadler's Wells Theater in 1792.

Why he and his family decided to leave London is not known. Perhaps such friends as Alexander Reinagle, James Hewitt, George Schetky, and Rayner Taylor, who had already emigrated, convinced them that greater financial opportunities were available in America.[5] Benjamin settled in Philadelphia in May of 1793 and was soon joined by his father, mother, and younger brother, Thomas.[6] Within a short time, they opened three musical repositories: Benjamin in Philadelphia (1793) and New York (1794) and Joseph and Thomas in Baltimore (1794).[7] The Carrs sold music, musical instruments, and other items and advertised themselves as music printers, importers, and instrument makers.[8] Joseph, unlike many early American publishers, was an expert engraver and combined his musical knowledge with his publishing skill to bring forth a product of good quality. Benjamin was also trained as an engraver, but whether or not he did his own engraving in America is purely speculative.[9] The Carrs were prolific publishers and for a few years

completely dominated the trade in the above cities. They offered a wide variety of music by American and European composers—primarily British composers and those, such as Haydn and Pleyel, whose music was popular in England. Joseph ran the Baltimore business until shortly before he died in 1819; then Thomas assumed control. Benjamin Carr sold the New York store to James Hewitt in 1797, and in 1800, he sold the Philadelphia repository. From about 1803 to about 1811, Carr and George Schetky jointly operated a music store in Philadelphia. Once again, between 1822 and ca. 1829, Carr was active in the trade but on a sporadic basis.[10]

Carr resumed his career as a performer as soon as the Philadelphia repository was firmly established. Philadelphia was then in the forefront as a cultural center where a relatively high level of musical activity was sustained. Private music-making was thriving, and the theater was flourishing with productions of English imports and new American works.[11] Many accomplished professional musicians resided in or visited the city and gave programs for the public in concert halls, churches, and outdoor gardens.[12] Carr made his debut in Philadelphia as a singer in the initial concert of a subscription series (of which he was one of the managers) held at Oeller's Hotel, 8 April 1794.[13] His repertoire in this and in the remaining concerts in the series mirrored that of the typical London program in which glees and solo numbers by Handel, Webbe, Hook, Storace, and other English composers were presented. How frequently Carr performed his own music in the various public concerts in which he participated cannot be determined. Concert programs of the time rarely give complete information; for example, one number on the program for 29 April 1794 merely states "Song, Mr. Carr," meaning that the song was performed by but not necessarily composed by Carr.[14] Even without verification, one presumes that Carr sang and played his own compositions in both public and private concerts.

In September of 1794, Carr made his American stage debut as actor-singer in the Old American Company's production of Thomas Arne's *Love in a Village*. A critic noted that Carr's portrayal of Young Meadows met with "universal applause" but suggested that he needed more practice as an actor.[15] Carr's singing and musicianship in this and in other roles continued to be praised, but his acting met with persistent criticism, and he abandoned the theater in the summer of 1795. Carr nevertheless pursued a concert career in Philadelphia and New York until about 1800; his public performances thereafter as a singer or pianist are infrequent. He most likely relinquished this facet of his career in favor of his increasing duties as church musician, conductor, and organist—fields in which he was acknowledged to be pre-eminent.[16]

Although an Episcopalian, Carr served as organist and choir director in both Episcopal and Roman Catholic churches. His most significant positions were in two of Philadelphia's largest and most prominent churches: St. Augustine's Roman Catholic Church from 1801 to 1831 and St. Peter's Episcopal Church from 1816 to 1831.[17] Carr was also organist at St. Joseph's Roman Catholic Church (appointed some time prior to 1801), and he served in that same capacity at St. Mary's Roman Catholic Church between 1807 and 1811. On occasion, he directed programs of sacred music in other churches, such as St. Luke's Church in the Germantown section of the city.

As a dedicated church musician, Carr's first mission was to improve the quality of the music being performed. He was restricted by the limitations of his relatively untrained choirs, yet he succeeded in elevating the caliber of music and in encouraging part-singing—mainly in three voice-parts.[18] He wrote various types of sacred works ranging from simple hymns to masses; made arrangements of standard works—"No choir . . . should be without Handel's *Messiah*," he said;[19] and compiled several collections of religious music that were put to practical use.[20] Copies of his *Masses, Vespers, Litanies*, for example, sold well not only in Philadelphia but in a number of American, English, and Scottish cities.[21] The transatlantic crossing of an American publication at that time was especially noteworthy. In addition to works for choir, Carr composed solo songs of a religious nature for church, school, and home use. A sampling is included in the present anthology.

Another of Carr's endeavors as a church musician was to raise the performance level. Good choral singing was established in Philadelphia primarily through Carr's initiative, and St. Augustine's became a major center for the performance of sacred music. One of the highlights of Carr's career took place in that church on 20 June 1810 when he, assisted by Rayner Taylor and George Schetky, directed a concert that was heralded as "the greatest musical event that had occurred up to that time in Philadelphia."[22] The ambitious program, featuring selections by Handel, Haydn, Pergolesi, Carr, and others, was performed by soloists, a choir of thirty-four members, and an unusually large orchestra of fifty-three instrumentalists.

In the secular area, too, Carr enthusiastically promoted cultural activites. His championship of American music is well documented in his correspondence with John Rowe Parker, publisher and editor of *The Euterpeiad*.[23] In one letter, Carr contends that "the music of this country should be particularly noticed and cherished,"[24] and in another, he gently chides Parker for devoting so much space in his journal to European music, thereby neglecting "domestic musicians."[25] As a result of his desire to inform the public about musicians who had distinguished themselves in America, Carr wrote a series of unsigned biographical sketches for *The Euterpeiad*; they appear under the heading of "Musical Reminiscences" beginning in January of 1822. His biographies of such figures as Rayner Taylor, Alexander Reinagle, George Gillingham, Georgina Oldmixon, Dolly Broadhurst, and others, provided first-hand information that is still of value today.[26]

Carr was persistent in encouraging greater involvement of the general citizenry in the support of serious music, but he was often frustrated in his efforts. He complained to Parker that "Philadelphia is very barren of any thing like public spirit as it relates to Music."[27] On another occasion, he wrote that the city has "a blaze of talent" and one must "stir the public mind into respect for musical people."[28] To that end, Carr's most worthwhile and lasting contribution was as one of the founders and directors of the Musical Fund Society, the oldest musical organization in America in continuous existence. The Society was established in 1820 to provide financial assistance to needy musicians and to cultivate musical taste through concerts sponsored by the Society. Carr remained active not only as a manager and trustee of the Society but also as a conductor and orchestrator. The records show that the Society was truly appreciative of Carr's administrative skill and his dedication to the aims of the organization.[29]

A pursuit to which Carr devoted much of his time and for which he received considerable recognition was as a teacher of voice, piano, and organ. His most famous pupil was Mrs. French, who achieved distinction as one of the finest American singers of the early nineteenth century; Carr took great pride in her success. She began her studies with Carr when she was Miss Halveran, a pupil in Mrs. Rivardi's Seminary for Young Ladies, and her lessons were on an almost daily basis.[30] Another of Carr's pupils was Benjamin Cross, a noted Philadelphia singer, organist, teacher, and conductor. Other pupils known to have had professional careers were Eliza Taws and Miss H. C. Taws, both singers. The large majority of Carr's pupils, however, were amateurs—young ladies who learned to sing and play the piano.[31] For them and for the public at large, Carr wrote and published instruction manuals: the *Analytical Instructor for the Piano Forte* (1826) and two for voice that are discussed below under Performance Practice. He also composed a number of didactic works for the piano, such as his *Six Progressive Sonatinas, Preludes for the Piano Forte, Musical Bagatelles,* and *Applicazione addolcita*.

Carr is particularly remembered today as one of America's early composers of opera. His most successful was *The Archers, or the Mountaineers of Switzerland*. The opera, which is based on the William Tell legend, was first presented by the members of the Old American Company in New York on 18 April 1796.[32] Carr's music and the libretto, which was by William Dunlap, were received "with great applause" and additional performances were given.[33] The text has survived, but the music, except for a rondo, a march, and two short songs, has been lost. (One of the extant songs is in the present anthology.)

Carr's output for the stage was prodigious during his first years in America. In a catalog of his own compositions that he compiled before 1800,[34] he listed five operas (including the one written in England), accompaniments to fourteen operas,[35] four overtures, and incidental music for other theatrical productions. (Dramatic presentations were usually performed with the addition of musical numbers at that time.) Carr also wrote the music for seven pantomimes, including *The Caledonian Frolic* (1795), which received frequent performances in Philadelphia, Baltimore, New York, Hartford, and Boston.[36] With the exception of several songs, a piano version of his greatly admired *Federal Overture* (a medley of patriotic and familiar songs),[37] and the above-mentioned operatic excerpts, the theatrical music has been lost.[38]

The large body of secular music still in existence consists primarily of songs (discussed in the section below) and pieces for the piano. The latter encompasses sonatas, variations, rondos, medleys, dances, technical studies, a battle piece, and other miscellaneous works.[39] Carr also wrote a few compositions for harp, a duet for two harpsichords, and preludes, voluntaries, and other works for organ. Furthermore, he arranged a number of compositions for flute, violin, clarinet, or guitar. One such instance is his arrangement of volume one of his *Musical Journal for the Piano Forte* as *Musical Journal for the Flute or Violin* (1800).

It is a matter of record that Carr was highly regarded by his contemporaries for both his professional accomplishments and his personal attributes. After Carr's death on 24 May 1831, the Musical Fund Society had the following epitaph engraved on his tombstone in St. Peter's churchyard:

> Charitable, without ostentation, faithful and true in his friendships, with the intelligence of a man he united the simplicity of a child. In testimony of the high esteem in which he was held, this monument is erected by his friends and associates of the Musical Fund Society of Philadelphia.

He has been appropriately described as the "leader in every worth-while musical movement in Philadelphia, a man of large and wholesome influence."[40] Benjamin Carr never married and he left his estate to his brother and to Thomas's children, whose descendants have maintained an interest in music to the present day.

The Music

Benjamin Carr's compositional skill is clearly demonstrated in the song. In this genre, he surpassed other American composers of his generation, such as Alexander Reinagle, Rayner Taylor, or James Hewitt,[41] in sensitivity to text, lyricism, and overall artistry. Factors contributing to his achievements, no doubt, were his own experience as a performer and teacher, his knowledge of the voice, his natural lyrical gift, his training in composition, his considerable keyboard ability, and his appreciation of good literature.

Carr composed songs throughout his professional career and produced a substantial body of compositions that range from simple ballads to bravura arias; he even approached the realm of the art song at times. The exact number of songs that Carr composed is impossible to ascertain. That some have been lost is evident from the titles of unlocated songs listed in his previously mentioned early catalog (see note 34) and in advertised concert programs. This writer has located several unpublished manuscripts and seventy-one published songs, almost all of

which were issued by the Carr family in Baltimore or Philadelphia.[42] With few exceptions, the published music has survived. Sizable collections are housed in the libraries listed below under Sources.

In addition to writing original works, Carr also arranged a number of folk and popular songs and prepared his own editions of songs and arias by European composers. These arrangements are not included in the above total nor have they been chosen as selections in the present anthology. Carr always acknowledged on the sheet music if he were responsible for composing or arranging a composition; therefore, an anonymous piece published by Carr that simply states "composed expressly for these Numbers" should not be attributed to him.

Carr's songs vary in length, ranging from one to twelve pages. He issued them in individual numbers, in small sets of from three to six songs, and in extended series, both subscription and non-subscription. The small sets include: *Three Ballads from Shakespeare* (pub. 1794), *Four Ballads* (1794), *Three Ballads* (1799), *Six Ballads from the Poem of the Lady of the Lake* (1810), *Carr's Canzonettes* (1824), and *Carr's Sacred Airs* (1830). His major subscription series was the *Musical Journal for the Piano Forte* (1800–1804), published by his father in Baltimore.[43] The title is misleading because the series alternates piano compositions with vocal works accompanied by the piano. (Most of the vocal works were written so that they could also be played as piano solos.) Totaling approximately 500 pages, the *Musical Journal*, over a five-year period, offered a diverse selection of 120 original compositions and arrangements representing more than seventy-five European and American composers.[44] Carr was responsible for determining the contents and for editing or composing many of the works. He was particularly concerned with elevating taste and with acquainting the public with the best contemporary music. But in addition, Carr was an astute business man, and he was able to produce a series that would capture the public's interest. Others had tried to establish similar subscription series in America, but Carr's was the first to survive beyond the initial year. Compositions from the series were also sold separately through music stores in many American cities, and the entire series was reissued by Carr and Schetky in 1806 or 1807.

Carr's second large-scale series, called *Musical Miscellany in Occasional Numbers*, was published in Baltimore from 1812 to 1821 (or 1822) and in Philadelphia from 1822 to 1825 (or 1826).[45] Carr no longer wished to commit himself to a regular subscription series, and he issued the eighty-six vocal and keyboard works at irregular intervals. In concept, the *Miscellany* is similar to the *Musical Journal* in that it reflects the repertoire then popular in England, features Carr as composer and arranger, and offers a limited number of compositions by Carr's American contemporaries.

The songs in the above-mentioned series and in the individual issues served as parlor music for amateurs, chiefly for young ladies with soprano voices. (According to the social mores of the time, women, rather than gentlemen, sang and played the piano.) The melodies are written in the treble clef, and the tessituras range from medium-high to high. In certain instances, the songs were written for specific occasions: a heading may inform us, for example, that a particular song was first performed by the young ladies of Mrs. Mallow's Academy or Mrs. Rivardi's Seminary.[46] A number of Carr's songs were associated with the theater or concert stage (four are included in the present anthology), and as an inducement to the buying public, the name of the performer is given in the heading. Carr's music was sung by most of the leading artists of the day, many of whom had previously attained fame on the London stage. Performers mentioned in the headings of the published songs and in concert programs include the following: Dolly Broadhurst, Mrs. Burke (formerly Mrs. Marshall), Mrs. French, Mrs. Green, Arabella Brett Hodgkinson, Elizabeth Jefferson, Georgina George Oldmixon, Mary Wrighton Pownall, Miss H. C. Taws, Mrs. Williamson, John Darley, Jr., William [John?] Darley (a.k.a. John Darley, Sr.), John Hodgkinson, and Joseph Tyler. (Note that the majority of vocalists are women.)

When performed on the stage, songs were traditionally accompanied by an orchestra. In their published versions for the domestic market, the accompaniment would be suitably adapted to the piano or occasionally the harp. In the eighteenth century, songs were normally printed on two staves with an interlinear text so that the right hand would double the melody line and the left would have an easy harmonic bass pattern. The amateur could readily accompany herself and still maintain the pitch. Additional notes could be added by the more accomplished pianist. Most of Carr's early songs, for instance eleven of the seventeen songs by him in the *Musical Journal,* were written in this fashion. His remaining songs in that series were written on three staves, but the piano doubles the melodic line much of the time. The impetus for three-stave writing in England and America stems perhaps from Haydn's usage of a written-out right-hand part in his very popular collections of canzonets (1794 and 1795), three of which were published by Carr in Philadelphia in 1799.

Carr's first set of songs published in America, *Three Ballads from Shakespeare* (1794), was printed in the new manner on three staves.[47] By 1810 he used three staves almost exclusively and sometimes provided the type of independent and idiomatic accompaniment that would prove to be so essential to the future development of the art song. To appeal to performers of limited ability, he occasionally offered an easy two-stave version on the final page of a publication; "Why, Huntress, Why" (no. [5] in the present anthology) is one such example which was printed in two versions in the *Musical Journal.*

For the subject matter of his songs, Carr turned to themes prevalent around 1800: sentimental, pastoral, amorous, pathetic, religious, and ethnic topics. (The latter includes imitations of Scottish and Irish folk songs then very much in vogue.) With few exceptions, Carr avoided comic, satirical, topical, and patriotic themes, despite the Carr family's special association with the publication of patriotic music and the success of Carr's own nationalistic *Federal Overture.*

Pastoral songs glorifying nature and love were especially favored in eighteenth-century England and America. This subject is well represented in Carr's total output, and "Adieu Ye Streams That Sweetly Flow" (no. [20]) is typical of the genre. By the nineteenth century, interest in pastoral love diminished, and greater attention was given to sentimental, pathetic, and even morbid texts. Carr became fascinated with pathetic texts around 1800 and set a number of tragic ballads over the following decade. Several are in his *Musical Journal,* such as the sorrowful tales of "The Poor Flower Girl," "The Orphan Boy," "The Widow," who is homeless and freezes to death in the wintry cold, and "Poor Mary," whose husband is murdered by robbers and dies at her feet. (Since the music that Carr composed for these poems fails to convey the intense emotions expressed by the words, this group of songs has not been included in the present anthology.)

For his settings from Sir Walter Scott's *Lady of the Lake* in 1810, Carr selected plaintive verses, such as the lament of "Coronach" and the songs of "Mary" and "Blanche of Devan," both of whose lovers die. Carr apparently wearied of morbid content, and after 1810 he concentrated primarily on pastoral, sentimental, and religious themes and on ballads harking back to the romanticized age of chivalry. Carr's only non-traditional text is in "The History of England," published in about 1814 in the *Musical Miscellany* series.[48] "The History" is a lengthy, didactic, and rather humorous song that traces the history of England from 800 to 1776; the work relies on cleverly inserted familiar and appropriate tunes.

Carr was well educated and maintained an awareness of current creative literature. Poets represented in his songs, aside from Scott and Shakespeare, include such English, Irish, and Scottish writers as Sir Thomas Moore, Robert Southey, Felicia Hemans, Amelia Opie, Robert Bloomfield, Thomas Campbell, Thomas Holcroft, and John Carr. Benjamin Carr also set texts by American poets, especially those affiliated with the theater. American writers represented in the present anthology are: William Dunlap, playwright, producer, historian, artist, and librettist of *The Archers;* John Edmund Harwood, actor, poet, and librettist, who was known to have been in Philadelphia in 1793 as a performer in Thomas Wignell's New Company; James Gates Percival, a physician and prolific writer of poetry, who was often called the "American Bard"; and David Paul Brown, a Philadelphia lawyer and playwright.

The poetry that Carr selected for his songs is of variable quality, and his choice has a direct bearing on the artistry of the finished product. Among the secular works, Carr's finest inspirations are based upon texts from Shakespeare and Sir Walter Scott. Some of these settings may be considered early examples of art song in America due to the insightful text interpretation and to the more significant role of the accompaniment. This small repertoire of serious music was obviously not intended for the broadest possible public but rather for professional musicians and for the more literate connoisseurs among the amateur performers. In his later years, Carr's approach was more utilitarian, and he tended to favor sentimental ballads over great literature. His settings of anonymous verses and of poems by contemporary writers other than Scott are generally less sophisticated, easier to perform, and of a more popular nature. The intrinsic value of the music lies more in the lyricism than in the integration of words and music or the intellectual content.

Carr and his American contemporaries were strongly influenced by British models, especially the ballads that were written for presentation in the English theaters and pleasure gardens. The lilting songs of Samuel Arnold, William Shield, Charles Dibdin, James Hook, Henry Bishop, and others were widely published in America and formed the basis of both the professional and amateur singer's repertoire. Also influential were the cantabile songs and brilliant arias of Italian composers such as Paisiello and Giordani, whose music was well known in England and America. Although individual differences existed among the various English composers, their vocal works tended to be either simple ballads or, to a lesser extent, florid arias. Their songs featured attractive melodies, regular rhythms, diatonic harmonies, major keys, and strophic form. This description also holds true for the majority of Carr's songs and for those of his American colleagues.

The Present Anthology

The works by Carr selected for the present anthology are limited to solo songs (although Carr did compose a small number of duets and trios) and, with two exceptions (no. [4] and no. [19]), to songs that were originally written on three staves with independent accompaniments. His settings of verses by Shakespeare and Scott are particularly featured, but representative examples of his other secular and sacred songs are also included. The songs are presented in chronological order ranging from the Shakespeare ballads to the final posthumous publication of 1832.[49] Each composition selected for the present edition was first issued in one of the sets or series mentioned above, with the exception of "As Pants the Hart" (no. [18]) and the final four songs in the anthology, which are based upon manuscript sources.

Although they were evidently composed about the same time, *Three Ballads from Shakespeare* (nos. [1]–[3]) were probably not conceived by Carr as a unified group.[50] "Take, Oh, Take Those Lips Away" (no. [2]), a ballad whose lyrics have inspired numerous composers, is the most ambitious and challenging of the three. This song's spacious melodic line, which has a range of almost two octaves (d' to b"-flat), shows strong dependence upon the aria style of Mozart, as does the song's extensive reliance upon appoggiaturas for both expressive and decorative purposes.[51] The well-shaped and rhythmically varied melody is one that is sensitive to both the meter and the general meaning of the poetry. The word "love" (m. 38), which serves as the song's central climax, is accentuated melodically, rhythmically, dynamically, and harmonically. (The diminished-seventh chord in this measure makes one of its rare appearances in Carr's early songs.) The octave passages and widely spaced chords in the accompaniment (mm. 29–36) reach out for the sound of an orchestra, and one may speculate that the song was also performed on the stage with an orchestral accompaniment.

In "Tell Me Where Is Fancy Bred" (no. [3]) Carr preserves the poetry by limiting text repetition, by adhering to a strict syllabic setting, and by using a through-composed form. The shifts in metrical arrangement (from trochaic to iambic), the short recitative passage, and the syncopated phrase endings (mm. 16 and 18) give additional declamatory emphasis. The piano accompaniment consistently doubles the melody, yet it contributes vital poetic illustrations with its sturdy chords after "reply" (mm. 19–20) and its imitations of the reverberating bells in the prelude and again at the conclusion of the song (mm. 33–40).

"When Icicles Hang by the Wall" (no. [1]) is the weakest of the set.[52] The song's melody takes precedence over the text, resulting in distortions of the poetic meter and accentuation of unimportant words, such as "and" in m. 11. The word "blows" in m. 8 is depicted by a rising slur, but the pattern is vocally awkward, and when that pattern is repeated in the following two measures, it is unrelated to the text. The modulation to the dominant key in m. 11 is too abrupt. Overall, the song lacks the coherence and the graceful flow that is generally associated with Carr's vocal style.

Carr's fourth Shakespeare setting, "Shakespeare's Willow" (no. [4]), was printed in volume one of the *Musical Journal* (1800). It is based on a very free adaptation of the text of Desdemona's song in *Othello*, act 4, scene 3. Carr approaches the poem with care. He successfully captures the haunting quality of the verses and faithfully follows the shifting metrical construction. Particularly striking are the crisp Scotch snap rhythms on the word "willow." This song is one of the few by Carr that is in a minor key. Also uncommon is the instability of the tonality that wavers between E and A minor and G major. Another unusual aspect of the song is its lack of a prelude or postlude.[53]

"Why, Huntress, Why" (no. [5]), in volume two of the *Musical Journal* (1800–1801),[54] has received considerable attention in recent years because it is one of the few surviving examples from Carr's opera *The Archers*.[55] In the opera, the song is performed by Arnold Melchthal (sung by Joseph Tyler), who is in love with Rhodolpha. He expresses his disapproval of her dressing as a huntress and her determination to fight alongside the men. This is the first song in the present anthology known to have been performed on the stage. (No evidence exists that the Shakespeare songs were associated with theatrical productions or the concert stage.) "Why, Huntress, Why" lacks the intimacy of "Shakespeare's Willow" and exhibits characteristics often associated with aria style. It displays (1) operatic flourishes, (2) a declamatory passage (beginning in m. 29), (3) extensive text repetition, (4) text illustration (melismas on "valued" in mm. 9 and 22 and a modulation to the minor mode in the middle section to express the fear of death in mm. 29–39), (5) a strong climax dramatized by the octave leap and colorful augmented-sixth chord in m. 37, and (6) a hint of the da capo aria form with the return of the opening melody at the end. An especially attractive rhythmic feature of the song is the contrast between duple and triple groupings.

In 1810 Sir Walter Scott published his narrative poem about the Scottish Highlands, *The Lady of the Lake*. It created a sensation, and within months, thousands of copies were sold in England and America. Carr's response was immediate. The year the poem was issued, Carr set to music and published as a subscription series *Six Ballads from the Poem of the Lady of the Lake*, Op. 7.[56] (Nos. [6]–[8] in the present anthology are from *Six Ballads*.) Although Scott himself had no ear for music and could scarcely sing or whistle a tune, he had the gift for writing lyric poetry. The ballads interpolated within his narrative tale inspired not only Carr but many other composers. Ellen's songs, "Hymn to the Virgin," subtitled "Ave Maria," and "Soldier, Rest!" are the best known of Scott's ballads, since both were set to music by Franz Schubert in 1825, fifteen years after Carr's settings.

In "Soldier, Rest!" (no. [6]) Carr pictorializes recollections of the battle scene through a stark, one-measure motive that is written in dotted martial rhythm and is performed in unison. The military motive alternates with a siciliana lullaby that represents the death of the soldier and the peace of eternal sleep. The first half of the song uses rising sequences to depict the tension of the battle. The return of the opening melody in m. 15 signals the death of the soldier. After the expressive, incomplete dominant-ninth harmony on "sleep" in m. 17, the vocal line gradually descends to the grave, leaving the accompaniment to portray "the rising sun" of the final verse and the heavenly rest.

"Hymn to the Virgin" (no. [7]) is undoubtedly Carr's finest song.[57] It offers a synthesis of words and music that is rarely found in either British or American song literature of the time. Carr's use of a modified strophic form gives further evidence of his concern with the text. Notice, for example, that Carr alters the rhythm and dynamics of the third verse to suit the text in m. 89 (compare with m. 11 of the first verse), and he uses a downward leap on "bow" in m. 94 (compare with m. 16 of the first verse). Carr allows the music to follow the natural accents of the poetry but not in a rigid manner. (The poetry itself provides diversity by shifting from dactylic to trochaic meter.) Carr varies the rhythmic values so that each phrase is entirely compatible not only with the poetic meter but also with the emotion expressed in the text; the resulting melodic style may thus change from lyric to dramatic to declamatory. Important words are stressed through brief embellishments or harmonic color, as with "despair" in mm. 14 and 15. The written-out embellishments, which become more intense and extended as the song progresses, are gracefully conceived and avoid the mechanical patterns of certain earlier songs.[58] The accompaniment is often independent of the vocal line and aids in interpreting the text: it depicts the angelic Virgin, with its arpeggiated chords for either harp or piano; it converses with the voice in mm. 20–21 and 24–25; and it introduces a descending tetrachord pattern in m. 7 that apparently symbolizes Ellen's plea. The pattern recurs frequently to unify the piece. But most striking of all in this work is its long-breathed, gently molded melodic line. The phrase beginning in m. 7, for example, has been aptly described as "the most touchingly beautiful phrase in all early American song."[59] Upton considers "Hymn to the Virgin" the beginning of art song in America,[60] and Hitchcock calls it "perhaps the most impressive American song before Foster's best."[61]

"Blanche of Devan" (no. [8]) adopts a pseudo-recitative style. The work is stripped of decorative aspects, and the musical elements—the austere declamatory line, the intense repeated patterns, the Spartan accompaniment, the metrical contrasts, the dramatic leaps—all focus attention on the tragedy expressed in the lyrics.

In 1813 Scott published another narrative poem, *Rokeby*, based upon English history at the time of the Civil War. Once again Carr was aware of the quality of Scott's verses and was quick to capitalize upon the poem's success in his *Four Ballads from the Celebrated New Poem of Rokeby*, Op. 10, published in the *Musical Miscellany* series (1813).[62] The songs were made available as individual numbers or as a set. The *Rokeby* ballads are illustrative of Scott's investigation and re-creation of the folk ballad style. In setting the verses to music, Carr approached them in a much less sophisticated manner than in his setting of *The Lady of the Lake* ballads. He did not aspire toward the art song, but, like Scott, he attempted to approximate the unpretentiousness and directness of the folk ballad.

The three ballads selected for the present anthology (nos. [9]–[11]) use the strophic design of the folk song, and although the second verse of "A Weary Lot Is Thine, Sweet Maid" (no. [10]) is written out, only two minor rhythmic changes are allowed. The simple harmonic plans stress tonic and dominant, and the melodic structures rely extensively upon the repetition and sequence of scalar and triadic patterns. (Less folklike are the occasional wide leaps and written-in embellishments, dynamics, articulations, fermatas, and tempo changes.) The accompaniment either doubles the voice (as in "A Weary Lot" and partly in "Allen-a-Dale," no. [11]) or employs arpeggiated chords imitative of the ballad singer's harp (as in "The Wandering Harper," no. [9], and "Allen-a-Dale").

In this set Carr deliberately avoids the musico-poetic relationship present in his more serious songs. In "The Wandering Harper," for example, he defies word-painting convention in the first verse by using awkward-sounding upward leaps of tenths to "gone" (m. 5) and "falling" (m. 7). Also inconsistent with the emotions expressed are the ascending melodic lines, which traditionally connote joy, in "A Weary Lot Is Thine." The charm, the flow, and the naturalness of the folk style is best reflected in "Allen-a-Dale," the most attractive of the ballads.

Other songs by Carr in the *Musical Miscellany* also demonstrate the increasing influence of the folk style. One such example is no. [12], "Thy Smiles Are All Decaying, Love" (ca. 1824), a sentimental strophic ballad whose swinging rhythmic motion and amiable melodic line convey a sense of spontaneity. The piano accompaniment is based on a standard harmonic pattern, and the phrase structure of the song is regular. (Many of Carr's earlier songs introduce irregular and extended phrases.)

In 1824 Carr issued his last collection of secular songs, Carr's Canzonetts, Op. 14.[63] (In the present anthology nos. [13]–[15] are from Carr's Canzonetts.) As a heading, canzonet had gained new popularity due to the success of Haydn's two sets of Six Original Canzonettas of 1794 and 1795. A canzonet is usually defined as a simple, cantabile song written in strophic form.[64] Both "Sea of Susa" (no. [15]) and "Noah's Dove" (no. [13]) in Carr's set fit the traditional description.

The Canzonetts, although not unified by poet, are linked through the use of similar subject matter—all but "Thou Faithful Guardian" pertain to love, an affable rather than a passionate love. Some evidence exists of an underlying cyclic concept in this set, as certain of the songs are related by recurring passages in the accompaniment: (1) the prelude to "The Minstrel Knight" (no. [14]) is based on the closing measures of "Noah's Dove"; (2) the scale passage in mm. 30 and 58 of "The Minstrel Knight" is similar to the scale patterns in the prelude, interlude, and postlude of "The Firefly"; (3) the arpeggiated chord and broken rhythms in the prelude to "Sea of Susa" appear again in mm. 43 to 45 of "The Minstrel Knight"; and (4) the repeated staccato chords of the prelude to the latter song are also featured in the prelude to "Thou Faithful Guardian."

The mood of each poem is reflected in the musical setting. The keyboard part in "Sea of Susa" (mm. 5–11 and 17–18) depicts the flowing sea. The accompaniment of "The Minstrel Knight," for which Carr recommends a harp, imitates the medieval harpist. In the latter song, Carr appropriately alters the accompaniment figure to match the words: vigorous rolled chords express "songs of war" in mm. 16–17 of the first verse, and light, staccato chords depict "in bard's disguise" in mm. 44–45 of the second verse. Throughout the collection, ornaments, fermatas, and tempo changes are utilized to provide poetic and musical emphasis.

During the latter part of his life, Carr was increasingly engrossed in his duties as a church musician. It is therefore not surprising that his last group of songs, Carr's Sacred Airs, Op. 16 (1830),[65] should be of a religious nature. The Sacred Airs (represented by nos. [16] and [17] here) are more diversified than the Canzonetts and may have been composed over a period of several years. "Song of the Hebrew Captive" (no. [16]) exists in a manuscript version that was probably used in performances prior to 1830.[66] Carr mentions in the heading of the published edition that the work was frequently sung by the "young ladies of Mrs. Rivardi's Seminary." Unlike the other numbers in this series, this work is a relatively lengthy heroic aria in oratorio style. To expand the work, Carr depends upon repetition of the text, which is taken from Psalm 137. He does not, however, resort to strict musical repetition. The recapitulation of the opening material (beginning in m. 81) is not presented as a literal reprise: the section that starts in m. 93 is curtailed, the accompaniment is varied and is assigned a more prominent role, and the conclusion is given greater emphasis.

The aria is somewhat reminiscent of "Hymn to the Virgin" (published twenty years earlier). Both feature sustained tones, flexible rhythms, a graceful melodic contour, and arpeggiated figuration in the accompaniment that is suitable for either harp or piano. Yet the aesthetic effect of the two compositions is different: "Hymn to the Virgin" is a subtle and intimate song, while "Song of the Hebrew Captive" is grandiose and dramatic.

"Hebrew Captive" has several illustrative passages: arpeggiated chords depict "the sounding lyre," descending diminished-fifth leaps express "when I forget" (mm. 61 and 63), and a rising melismatic scale portrays the word "glory" (m. 64). But not all of the florid passages are poetically inspired; observe, for instance, the incongruous use of melismas on the preposition "to" in mm. 68 and 71.

The accompaniment is an integral part of the setting. With its full chords, wide range, powerful octaves, and hand crossing, it is Carr's richest. Dynamics and articulation are carefully marked, and pedal indications are provided. The extended postlude further emphasizes the significant role of the accompaniment.

More typical of Carr's Sacred Airs as a whole is "An Autumnal Hymn" (no. [17]), a pastoral siciliana that is reflective rather than dramatic. In style, it is similar to the lyrical canzonets and to the sentimental parlor songs of the nineteenth century. The form is modified strophic, and the second stanza is altered so that the melody, harmony, and accompaniment assist in conveying the sentiments of the poem. (Compare mm. 37–41 to mm. 18–20 of the first stanza.) As in Carr's other late works, secondary-dominant and diminished-seventh chords are used more freely.

The last printed song and possibly the last composition that Carr composed was "As Pants the Hart" (no. [18]), published posthumously in 1832. "As Pants the Hart" is a metrical paraphrase of Psalm 42. It is set in ternary form and recalls the dramatic, bravura aria style of the Handelian era. The majestic, march-like first section provides a contrast to the more eloquent central section that is subdivided into a Recitative: Largo (in the parallel minor key) and a Larghetto (that returns to the tonic). Most striking in the Larghetto passage are the diminished-fourth leaps that depict the words "forlorn, forsaken" (mm. 42–44). The chronology of the published songs in the present anthology ends with this number. The remaining works in the anthology are based upon manuscript sources of which only one can be accurately dated.

In his capacity as a church musician, Carr was expected to provide music for funerals. One of his most famous compositions is the "Dead March and Monody," written for the memorial services honoring George Washington on 26 December 1799 at Old Zion Church and the Lutheran Church. A funeral work by Carr that is not mentioned in either the secondary literature or the bibliographic catalogs is "A Requiem" (no. [19]). The manuscript, discovered by the present writer in the Free Library of Philadelphia, is not in Carr's hand but is attributed to him in the heading. The work, according to the inscription, was "sung at the Funeral of Mr. [Thomas] Wignell," actor and manager of the New Company, who died on 21 February 1803. "A Requiem," which is written on two staves in a simple binary form, is probably typical of the funeral music of the time.

The final three songs (nos. [20]–[22]) in the present edition are scored for voice, flute, and violoncello, and are accompanied by piano in one instance and harp in two. The songs appear in a set of bound autograph manuscript partbooks that were donated to the Free Library of Philadelphia by Mrs. E. Paul Du Pont. The music is undated, and the partbooks for flute and violoncello bear the title *Armonia domestica;* the title page is missing from the piano-vocal book. The songs are especially valuable as examples of performance practice in the home around 1800. Whether Carr compiled the music books for an amateur group or for his own circle of friends, such as George Schetky, a fine cellist who shared Carr's home for a time and was his partner in a music store, is impossible to determine.

"Adieu Ye Streams That Sweetly Flow" (no. [20]) is a pastoral aria written in the eighteenth-century style. The music, in response to the imagery of the text, uses rippling chordal patterns, gentle sighing motives, and bird-like trills. The instrumental accompaniment, which assists in establishing the mood, provides motivic interplay with the voice and utilizes streams of lilting parallel thirds of the type so common in other works, such as "Hymn to the Virgin" and "Song of the Hebrew Captive." "Adieu Ye Streams" was probably never published; a printed version has not been located, and the song is not mentioned in the various bibliographic catalogs. It was most likely composed after Carr compiled his own catalog, but the musical style suggests that it is a fairly early work.

"When Nights Were Cold" (no. [21]), on a text by John Edmund Harwood, must have been a Carr favorite, since he included it (for voice and piano) in his *Four Ballads* (1794), a new edition of his *Three Ballads from Shakespeare,* and again in the third volume of his *Musical Journal* (1801–1802). According to Carr's own catalog, it was sung by some of the most prominent vocalists of the era: Miss Broadhurst, Mrs. Hodgkinson, Mrs. Oldmixon, Mrs. Pownall, and Mrs. Williamson. It is also one of the five known songs that Carr provided for the Philadelphia production of Samuel Arnold's *Children in the Wood* on 24 November 1794.

Carr's arrangement of "When Nights Were Cold" in *Armonia domestica* was most likely prepared after the version for piano and voice: the accompaniment is more suitable for the piano than for the harp, and the flute and violoncello parts add little that is new or significant. The manuscript, when compared with the printed version, does indicate that Carr made a few changes. The print opens with the voice unaccompanied, but the manuscript provides the customary prelude based upon the initial theme. The manuscript adds a written-out ornament to the fermata in the flute part (m. 22) and enriches the accompaniment (mm. 23–26)—all of the note values in this passage are halved, and broken patterns replace chords. The influence of Haydn's canzonets is clearly identifiable in this work. Beyond mere coincidence is the strong resemblance of the descending chromatic passage in mm. 27–30 to a similar passage in mm. 23–24 of Haydn's most familiar canzonet, "A Pastoral Song," also known as "My Mother Bids Me Bind My Hair" (1794).[67]

No. [22], "Ellen, Arise" (sometimes called "A Day of Harwoods"), was similarly set to a poem by J. E. Harwood and, like his "When Nights Were Cold," must have attained considerable popularity, for it was performed in the theaters in New York and Philadelphia by Miss Broadhurst, Mrs. Oldmixon, and both Mr. and Mrs. Hodgkinson. The climactic and dramatic treatment of the words "Ellen, arise" in mm. 23–28 probably captured the attention of both the singers and the audience. The song was published in a two-stave version for piano and voice in about 1798, with just a simple Alberti-bass accompaniment. The arrangement in *Armonia domestica* provides a more independent keyboard part, with full chords, octaves, and varied accompanying figures. As in the previous song, the flute and violoncello parts appear to be afterthoughts. The violoncello doubles the bass line, and the flute shines forth only in the brief interludes. For a comparison of the manuscript (piano and voice parts) and the printed edition, see Plates I and II.

Benjamin Carr assumed a significant role in the history of song-writing in America, and he attained the height of his career in 1810 with his imaginative and poetic setting of "Hymn to the Virgin" (no. [7]), which is undoubtedly the finest early American song. His remaining compositions may not have realized the potential for greatness expressed in this work, but overall his songs clearly illustrate his gift for writing graceful melodies well suited to the voice, his sensitivity to the imagery of the poetry, and his development of an independent and idiomatic accompaniment. In her study of American song literature, Grace D. Yerbury suggests that Carr combined the characteristics of three eighteenth-century American schools of song-writing. She defines them as "the Philadelphian with its conservative form and balanced harmonic and melodic design; the New York with its reduction of means and expansion of form; and the Bostonian with its cultural purpose . . . and appeal to the amateur."[68] Carr was restricted by his own pragmatic nature and by the practical necessity of providing functional music for a growing public of amateurs who were desirous of culture yet limited in ability and who looked upon music as a means of providing social pleasure rather than an intellectual challenge. Carr was sometimes frustrated in his endeavors, but he persisted in his many activities as a composer, church musician, and publisher to uplift the artistic level of music in America.

Performance Practice

In the late eighteenth and early nineteenth centuries, singers in America were expected to embellish arias, songs, and ballads, but in a tasteful manner. Carr's most famous pupil, Mrs. French, was praised by John Rowe Parker for her discretion in the art of ornamentation. He noted in one review that her "embellishments never lead the ear too great a distance from her melody."[69] In another article, he described her style of ornamentation as "vigorous, yet delicate, fertile, and luxuriant."[70]

The traditional place for ornamentation in an aria in ternary form was on the return of the opening section. Carr provides a typical illustration in "As Pants the Hart" (no. [18]) by writing out the cadenzas in mm. 70 and 75. Successive verses of a strophic song were also frequently embellished. An example by Carr is in "Hymn to the Virgin" (no. [7]), in which the melodic line, in a few places, is gently decorated in verses two and three but without destroying the character of the song.

In his *Analytical Instructor*, Carr suggests that the performer interpolate an embellishment or cadenza at the fermata, especially if "AD LIBITUM is added."[71] Examples of such usage may be found in no. [11], "Allen-a-Dale" (m. 12), and no. [16], "Song of the Hebrew Captive" (m. 28). In numerous songs, Carr may write out a brief embellishment at the fermata (without inserting *ad libitum*) as in [14], "The Minstrel Knight" (mm. 26 and 54), and no. [15], "Sea of Susa" (m. 19). There are also many instances in which the performer should probably improvise an embellishment at the fermata, as for example in m. 37 of "Why, Huntress, Why" (no. [5]).

Carr's recommendation that preludes and postludes (called "symphonies") should be added to songs that have been printed without them has already been noted. That he preferred a richer and more varied accompaniment than was in the printed score has been illustrated in the above comparison of the manuscript and printed versions of "Ellen, Arise" (no. [22]).

Additional performance practice information is available in Carr's two instruction manuals on the art of singing. The first, *Vocal Instruction* (n.d.), is a five-page tutor for beginners that explains the fundamentals of music reading and presents vocal exercises in various keys in the treble clef that illustrate rhythmic patterns, intervals, and embellishments. In about 1811, Carr compiled the second method book, *Lessons and Exercises in Vocal Music*.[72] This sixty-page volume is more substantial; it contains vocal exercises, solfeggio practice, instruction in diction and vocal technique, and numerous musical illustrations. Although not original in concept, the manual provides worthwhile information pertaining to the type of musical instruction given to the amateur singer of the time. Carr's explanation of the art of ornamentation is applicable to the songs in the present anthology. Several excerpts from *Lessons and Exercises* follow below.

In his directions to the singer, Carr stresses "the absolute necessity of keeping the mouth open, throwing out the Voice, sustaining the Tones," and avoiding "Gutteral, Nasal, and Dental sounds." Regarding diction, he cautions: "When two or more sounds occur to one syllable, do not dwell on the Consonant . . . but let the passage be on the Vowel, and if concluding with a Consonant do not let it be heard 'till the very last." He gives further advice as to the proper treatment of vowel and consonant sounds: "avoid harshness in pronouncing the K," and "the broad A and the soft O will be preferable where those Vowels occur."[73]

Carr observes "that many a Lady has complained of her inability to sing a song to her own satisfaction." His own experience has indicated that the problem is usually not with the singing but with the accompaniment. He states that the "manner in which Songs are too often accompanied is very reprehensible . . . with false notes particularly in the bass, blundering passages, [and] hurried and imperfect symphonies."[74]

Under embellishments or "graces," Carr illustrates different types of turns, both prepared and unprepared, noting that "the sharp Turn is the most usual, whether particularly marked or not."[75] In his published songs, Carr usually writes out the turn, as in "Sea of Susa" (no. [15], mm. 8 and 19), "Hymn to the Virgin" (no. [7], m. 8), and "A Weary Lot Is Thine" (no. [10], mm. 3, 5, 10). One of the few works in which he uses the symbol for the turn is "Song of the Hebrew Captive" (no. [16], mm. 28 and 64).

Carr recommends that the trill or "shake" be practiced slowly, since a good trill is necessary for every singer, although he remarks that the trill "is now more sparingly used than formerly."[76] (The many trills in "Adieu Ye Streams That Sweetly Flow," no. [20], is another indication that the song is probably an early one.) In the various musical examples in *Lessons and Exercises*, the trills begin on the main note. For the termination of the trill, "Grace Notes are only to be added upon Pauses" (meaning fermatas), and these grace notes should be performed slowly to "make an elegant termination."[77] An example is in m. 15 of "Hymn to the Virgin."

For the appoggiatura, Carr gives the traditional explanation that it should be performed on the beat, usually receiving one-half of the following note value and even "somewhat more." Carr complains that the appoggiatura is often sung too quickly and advises that the note be stressed and be performed in the character of the piece.[78] The appoggiaturas in mm. 15 and 20 in "Ellen, Arise" (no. [22]) illustrate his point.

To clarify the proper method of singing and interpreting the ornaments, Carr devotes a major portion of his *Lessons and Exercises* to two versions of "The Vi'let Nurs'd in Woodland Wild," a two-part aria consisting of an Andantino and a bravura Allegro. The first version, which is printed on two staves, includes written-out embellishments, breath marks, and instruction in diction. For example, on the second syllable of the word "perfume" (mm. 30–31), Carr suggests that the singer should "be careful of a disagreable [sic] hum upon this syllable," and on "pride" (m. 10), he recommends that one should "sing this vowel with a more open pronunciation than in reading."[79] He urges the performer to practice the first version of the aria "well on a Piano Forte in good tune, playing its embellishments and all that is written in the proper time, till it is correctly perfect."[80] The second version of the aria, which is printed on three staves, is to be used after the first version has been mastered. Numerals that refer to the written-out instructions in the first version are inserted above the notes.

The second version of Carr's "Vi'let Nurs'd," from his *Lessons and Exercises*, Op. 8, comprises the Appendix of the present anthology. Accents and breath marks have been added from its first version in the *Lessons*. The Key to Symbols in this Appendix gives the interpretation of numbered ornaments and signs as taken from Carr's first version of the song.

Editorial Methods

In the present anthology, modern conventions have been adopted for the notation, beaming, syllabification, and text underlay. Tempi, dynamics, accidentals, dots, rests, and other symbols added by the editor are enclosed in brackets. Redundant accidentals have been eliminated without comment. Editorial ties and slurs added by analogy with similar phrases or to facilitate underlay of subsequent verses are indicated by dashed lines. For nos. [4] and [19] a three-stave version has been editorially prepared from the two-stave versions of their respective primary sources.

The spelling, capitalization, and punctuation of all titles and verses in this edition reflect modern usage. If the title given by Carr differs in those respects from the one used in this edition, the original Carr title appears, enclosed in parentheses, in its respective entry under *Source Listings* in The Sources. In most instances, Carr omits or makes limited use of punctuation marks for the text underlay; he is usually more attentive in the added verses given at the end of the song. Wherever possible, the texts of Carr's songs have been compared with the verses in the original sources; that is, the Psalms and the works by Shakespeare and Scott. The punctuation and capitalization found in these sources is used in the present edition when omitted by Carr. Differences between those sources and the text as set by Carr are reported in the Critical Notes. Editorial corrections have very occasionally been made in Carr's texts, and these too are reported in the Critical Notes. For discrepancies in text between Carr's manuscript and printed versions of "When Nights Were Cold" (no. [21]) and "Ellen, Arise" (no. [22]), the manuscript text is used and the printed text is given in the Critical Notes.

Carr underlays only the first verse of a strophic song, with the exception of "Adieu Ye Streams That Sweetly Flow" (no. [20]). His format, including the numbering (or lack of numbering) of the additional verses, is followed in the present edition. In the additional verses, Carr at times provides the lines or phrases of the text that should be repeated, as in "The Wandering Harper" (no. [9]). When repeated text is omitted by Carr, the present editor has added such text in brackets to assist the performer. Cue-size notes and dashed slurs indicate alterations required in one or more of the additional verses.

The Sources

This section consists of two lists. The first list provides bibliographic expansions of the sigla used in the second list.

Sigla for Libraries and Private Collections

The locations of published editions and manuscript copies are indicated by the standard abbreviations for libraries and private collections as found in *New Serial Titles*.[81]

| ABHu | Arthur Billings Hunt—Alfred C. Berol Collection, Columbia University, New York |

CWU	C. W. Unger Collection, Pottsville, Pennsylvania
DLC	Library of Congress, Washington, D.C.
ES	Elliott Shapiro Collection, New York Public Library, New York
HFB	Harry F. Bruning Collection, Brigham Young University, Provo, Utah
JFD	James Francis Driscoll Collection, Newberry Library, Chicago, Illinois
LSL	Lester S. Levy Collection, Pikesville, Maryland and John Hopkins University, Baltimore, Maryland
MB	Boston Public Library, Boston, Massachusetts
McD-W	Josephine A. McDevitt and Edith A. Wright Collection, Free Library of Philadelphia, Philadelphia, Pennsylvania
MdHi	Maryland Historical Society, Baltimore, Maryland
MH	Harvard University, Cambridge, Massachusetts
MWA	American Antiquarian Society, Worcester, Massachusetts
NBuG	Grosvenor Reference Division, Buffalo & Erie County Public Library, Buffalo, New York
NHi	New York Historical Society, New York
NN	New York Public Library, New York
NRU-Mus	Sibley Music Library, Eastman School of Music, Rochester, New York
PHi	Historical Society of Pennsylvania, Philadelphia, Pennsylvania
PP	Free Library of Philadelphia, Philadelphia, Pennsylvania
PP-K	Edward I. Keffer Collection, Free Library of Philadelphia, Philadelphia, Pennsylvania
PU	University of Pennsylvania, Philadelphia, Pennsylvania
RPB	Brown University, Providence, Rhode Island
RPJCB	John Carter Brown Library, Providence, Rhode Island
SS	Saul Starr Collection, Indiana University, Bloomington, Indiana
ViW	College of William and Mary, Williamsburg, Virginia

Source Listings

The primary source for each of the works in the present anthology is given first in the list of sources that follows. For nos. [1]–[3] and [9]–[11], the earliest published editions are the primary sources. For nos. [21] and [22], the manuscript copies, which include parts for flute and violoncello, are the primary sources.

The song title appears first, with the spelling, punctuation, and capitalization reflecting modern usage. If Carr's original title differs in those regards, his version of the title appears enclosed in parentheses. If the title is lacking, the first line of the text is given. Each entry provides publication or manuscript information, RISM number (if available), locations of published editions or manuscript copies, and source of the text.

1. *When Icicles Hang by the Wall* (When Icicles hang by the wall). (In *Three Ballads from Shakespeare*, pp. 2–3) Philadelphia: Carr & Co., [1794]. Additional title page information: "From Shakespear's Love's Labour Lost." DLC, ES.

1a. ⸻ (In *Four Ballads*, pp. 2–3) Philadelphia: Carr & Co., [1794] (a new edition using the same plates). Additional title page information: "Three from Shakespeare, and one by Harwood, Composed & Respectfully inscribed to Mrs. Hodges, by Benjamin Carr." RISM: C 1241. DLC.

1b. ⸻ London: F. Linley [n.d.]. RISM: C 1253. PU.

1c. Untitled. First line: "When icicles hang by the wall." Autograph manuscript in Benjamin Carr's music book [1793]. (Notebook no. 159, pp. 50–51) ABHu.

Text: William Shakespeare, *Love's Labour's Lost*, act 5, scene 2.

2. *Take, Oh, Take Those Lips Away* (Take Oh! take those Lips away). (In *Three Ballads from Shakespeare*, pp. 4–5) Philadelphia: Carr & Co., [1794]. Additional title page information: "From Shakespear's Merchant of Venice." DLC, LSL, SS.

2a. ⸻ (In *Four Ballads*, pp. 4–5). See no. 1a above.

2b. Untitled. First line: "Take O take those lips away." Autograph manuscript. See no. 1c above (pp. 52–53).

Text: First verse, William Shakespeare, *Measure for Measure*, act 4, scene 1. (The source given by Carr is incorrect.) Second verse, attributed to John Fletcher.

3. *Tell Me Where Is Fancy Bred* (Tell me where is Fancy bred). (In *Three Ballads from Shakespeare*, pp. 6–7) Philadelphia: Carr & Co., [1794]. Additional title page information: "From Shakespear's Measure for Measure." ABHu, DLC, MWA.

3a. ⸻ (In *Four Ballads*, pp. 6–7). See no. 1a above.

3b. *Ballad from Shakespear*. First line: "Tell me where is fancy bred." Autograph manuscript. See no. 1c above (pp. 46–49). At the conclusion it is signed: "B Carr 17 Nov. 1793."

Text: William Shakespeare, *Merchant of Venice*, act 3, scene 2. (The source given by Carr is incorrect.)

4. *Shakespeare's Willow* (Shakespeares Willow). (In the *Musical Journal for the Piano Forte*, 1:22) Baltimore: J. Carr, [1800]. Two staves. Additional title page information: "My Mother had a Maid call'd BARBARIE: She was in Love; and he she lov'd forsook her and she prov'd mad. She had a Song of WILLOW an old thing 'twas, but it express'd her Fortune and she died singing it." DLC, ES, LSL, MdHi, NN, NRU-Mus, PP-K.

Text: William Shakespeare, *Othello*, act 4, scene 3 (paraphrased).

5. *Why, Huntress, Why* (Why huntress why). (In the *Musical Journal for the Piano Forte*, 2: 32–34) Baltimore: J. Carr, [1800–1801]. Three staves in A major followed by a simplified two-stave version "with an easy Accompaniment" in G major. Additional title page information:

"Sung by Mr. Tyler in the Opera of the Archers at the New York Theatre and by Mr. John Darley at the Concerts in Philadelphia. Published at the request of several Subscribers." DLC, LSL, NN, PP.

Text: William Dunlap, *The Archers, or the Mountaineers of Switzerland*.

6. *Soldier, Rest!* (Soldier rest). (In *Six Ballads from the Poem of the Lady of the Lake*, Op. 7, No. 2) Philadelphia: Carr and Schetky, [1810]. Copyright: 6 October 1810. Additional title page information: "Published in 6 Periodical Numbers." DLC, JFD, LSL, MH, NN, ViW.

Text: Sir Walter Scott, *The Lady of the Lake*, canto 1, stanzas 31–32.

7. *Hymn to the Virgin*, subtitled *Ave Maria*. (In *Six Ballads*, No. 3). See no. 6 above. Additional title page information: "NB: this Accompanyment will be found to be well adapted for the Harp, by previously tuning the D's flat, then playing it on the open strings in the key of A♭ major, using the Pedals as they are mark'd, wherever accidentals occur." DLC, JFD, MH, MdHi, NN, ViW.

Text: Sir Walter Scott, *The Lady of the Lake*, canto 3, stanza 29.

8. *Blanche of Devan*. (In *Six Ballads*, No. 4). See no. 6 above. DLC, JFD, LSL, MH, NN, ViW.

Text: Sir Walter Scott, *The Lady of the Lake*, canto 4, stanza 22.

9. *The Wandering Harper*. (In *Musical Miscellany in Occasional Numbers*, No. 9) Baltimore: J. Carr, [1813]. ABHu, CWU, DLC, LSL, MB, MWA, NN.

9a. ⸻ (In *Four Ballads from the Celebrated New Poem of Rokeby*, pp. 2–3) Baltimore: J. Carr, [ca. 1814]. (Reissued from the same plates).

Text: Sir Walter Scott, *Rokeby*, canto 5, stanzas 7 and 9.

10. *A Weary Lot Is Thine, Sweet Maid* (A Weary Lot is thine Sweet Maid). (In *Musical Miscellany*, No. 10). See no. 9 above. CWU, DLC, LSL, MWA, NN, PP-K.

10a. ⸻ (In *Four Ballads*, pp. 4–5). See no. 9a above.

Text: Sir Walter Scott, *Rokeby*, canto 3, stanza 28.

11. *Allen-a-Dale* (Allen A Dale). (In *Musical Miscellany*, No. 11). See no. 9 above. ABHu, CWU, DLC, JFD, LSL, MH, MWA, NHi, NN.

11a. ⸻ (In *Four Ballads*, pp. 6–8). See no. 9a above.

Text: Sir Walter Scott, *Rokeby*, canto 3, stanza 30.

12. *Thy Smiles Are All Decaying, Love* (Thy smiles are all decaing love). (In *Musical Miscellany*, No. 81) Philadelphia: B. Carr, [ca. 1824]. Additional title page information: "A Ballad." ABHu, NN, PP-K, PU.

Text: James Gates Percival, source unknown.

13. *Noah's Dove*. (In *Carr's Canzonetts*, Op. 14, No. 1) Philadelphia: B. Carr, [1824]. Additional title page information: "Entered according to Act of Congress the twelfth day of June 1824 by Benjamin Carr of the State of Pennsylvania. Canzonett. Sung by Mrs. Burke at the Public Concerts. Printed for the Composer, and sold at T. Carrs Music Store No. 132 South Second Street." ABHu, DLC, JFD, LSL, MdHi, MH, MWA, NN, PHi, PP-K.

Text: Author unknown.

14. *The Minstrel Knight.* (In *Carr's Canzonetts*, No. 3). See no. 13 above. Additional title page information: "With an Accompanyment for the Harp." ABHu, DLC, JFD, MWA, NBuG, NN, PHi, PP, PP-K, PU, RPB.

Text: Author unknown.

15. *Sea of Susa.* (In *Carr's Canzonetts*, No. 5). See no. 13 above. Additional title page information: "The Words translated from a Moorish Ballad." ABHu, DLC, LSL, NN, PHi, PP-K.

Text: Author unknown.

16. *Song of the Hebrew Captive,* subtitled *O Sion, O Jerusalem.* (In *Carr's Sacred Airs,* No. 1) Philadelphia: B. Carr, [1830]. Additional title page information: "Entered according to act of congress the 10th day of April 1830 by B. Carr of the state of Pennsylvania. Composed with an Accompaniment for the Harp or Piano Forte. This Air was originally composed for, and frequently sung at the Concerts of Sacred Music performed by the young ladies of Mrs. Rivardi's Seminary." ABHu, CWU, DLC, LSL, MdHi, NN, PP, PU.

16a. *From Psalm 137.* An autograph manuscript copy of *Song of the Hebrew Captive.* Nine pages. PP (Mahlon Bunting Knowles Collection, uncataloged).

Text: Psalm 137.

17. *An Autumnal Hymn.* (In *Carr's Sacred Airs,* No. 5). See no. 16 above. ABHu, CWU, DLC, LSL, NN, PP, PU.

Text: David Paul Brown, source unknown.

18. *As Pants the Hart.* Philadelphia: Published for T. Carr by Miller and Osbourn, [ca. 1832]. Additional title page information: "Composed for the Piano Forte by the late Benjamin Carr." LSL, MdHi, NN, PP-K.

Text: Psalm 42.

19. *A Requiem.* A single page manuscript written in an unidentified hand, [1803]. Two staves. Additional title page information: "Sung at the Funeral of Mr. Wignell. Composed by Mr. B. Carr." PP (uncataloged).

Text: Author unknown.

20. Untitled. First line: "Adieu ye streams that sweetly flow." (In *Armonia domestica,* No. 2). Three bound autograph manuscript partbooks, undated. One partbook is for voice and harp, with portions of the flute and violoncello parts in cue-size notes; the title page is missing. One partbook is for flute and another is for violoncello; each has *Armonia domestica* on the title page. The volumes were donated by Mrs. E. Paul Du Pont. PP (uncataloged).

Text: Author unknown.

21. Untitled. First line: "When nights were cold." (In *Armonia domestica,* No. 5). See no. 20 above, except that the voice and harp partbook in this case includes portions of the flute part only.

21a. *When Nights Were Cold* (When Nights were cold). (In *Four Ballads,* pp. 8–9). See no. 1a above. Additional title page information: "A favorite ballad." RISM: C 1254. DLC.

21b. ———— (In the *Musical Journal for the Piano Forte,* 3: 36–38) Philadelphia: B. Carr, [1801–1802] DLC, RPJCB, PP, PP-K.

21c. ———— (In *Musical Magazine,* 2: 60–61) Boston, [1802–1803]. Additional title page information: "An original song. Introduced in the Opera of The Children in the Woods [sic]."

Text: John Edmund Harwood, source unknown.

22. Untitled. Known as: *Ellen, Arise.* First line: "See from yon cottage window plays." (In *Armonia domestica,* No. 6). See no. 20 above, except that the accompaniment is for piano instead of harp.

22a. *Ellen, Arise* (Ellen Arise). Philadelphia: B. Carr, [ca. 1798]. Two staves. Additional title page information: "A Ballad. As Sung at the Philadelphia and New York Theatres by Mrs. Oldmixon & Mrs. Hodgkinson." RISM: C 1250. ABHu, DLC, HFB, JFD, LSL, McD-W, MH, NHi, NN, PP, PP-K, PU, RPB.

22b. ———— London: T. Jones & Co., [n.d.]. RISM: C 1251. NN.

Text: John Edmund Harwood, source unknown.

Critical Notes

The following notes refer to discrepancies between the present edition and the primary printed or manuscript source and between primary and secondary sources. Discrepancies between Scott's and Shakespeare's original text and Carr's versions are also cited. The conventional system of pitch designation is used, wherein c' indicates middle C, and so forth. M refers to measure, and RH and LH refer to the top and bottom staves of the piano or harp part.

[1] When Icicles Hang by the Wall

M. 15, third and fourth words are "is nipp'd" in Shakespeare. M. 20, LH, beat 1 word is a quarter-note. Mm. 20 and 21, beat 1 word is "who" in Shakespeare. The manuscript copy of the song is written on two staves. Notes are crossed out in a few instances, rests are often lacking, and the left-hand part is notated in a sketchy manner; for example, repeated patterns, as in mm. 6–9 and 25–27, are not always written out. Other significant discrepancies are as follows: M. 2, RH, beats 4 and 5 are eighth-note, eighth-rest. M. 5, voice, beats 1 and 2 are eighth-note, eighth-note. The second verse is lacking.

[2] Take, Oh, Take Those Lips Away

M. 9, second word is "O," and m. 18, second word is "the" in Shakespeare. Verse 2, line 3, last word is "grows" in Carr. The manuscript copy of the song is written on two staves and is notated in a sketchy manner. Rests and the lower note of chords are sometimes lacking, and note heads are not carefully placed on the staff. Dynamic markings and the second verse are lacking. Other discrepancies are as follows: M. 2, both hands, note 1 is a dotted quarter-note. M. 4, LH, note 1 is a dotted quarter-note. M. 23, voice, note 2 is c"-sharp. M. 50, RH, notes 2–7 are lacking; note 1 is a quarter-note and beat 2 is a quarter-rest. Two measures are inserted between mm. 50 and 51: RH, e'''-flat, d''', c''', b"-flat, a"-flat, g", f", quarter-note and six eighth-notes; LH, two-measure rest.

[3] Tell Me Where Is Fancy Bred

M. 21, "It is engend'red" in Shakespeare. M. 22, voice, note 2 is e'—editorially emended by analogy with both hands and with the manuscript copy (see Source Listings 3b). Discrepancies with the manuscript are as follows: M. 19, RH, beats 3 and 4, d' is added to the chords. M. 20, RH, beats 3 and 4, chords are d', f'-sharp, a', d". M. 23, RH, beat 1 is c'-natural; LH, beat 1 is c-natural. M. 36, voice, e", c", a', f"-sharp; RH, e", c", a', chord d" and f"-sharp; LH, e', c', a, f'-sharp. M. 37, voice and RH, note 2 is b'; LH, note 2 is b. M. 39, LH, note 4, and mm. 40 (all) and 41, notes 1–3, include the octave below. M. 41, both hands, beat 6 is sixteenth-rest, sixteenth-note chords.

[4] Shakespeare's Willow

The text is a free paraphrase of Shakespeare, and the differences are too numerous to list. In the primary source, the song is printed on two staves and lacks the customary prelude and postlude. The present edition includes an optional prelude and postlude in cue-size notes. The version of this song in Elwyn A. Wienandt, *The Bicentennial Collection of American Music* (Carol Stream, Ill., 1974), p. 240, is in error in interpreting the quarter-rest in m. 5, voice and RH, beats 4 and 5, as a'.

[5] Why, Huntress, Why

No variants.

[6] Soldier, Rest!

Mm. 5 and 18, second word is "not" in Scott. Verse 2, line 2, third word is "of" in Scott.

[7] Hymn to the Virgin. Ave Maria

In the heading, Carr says that "this Accompanyment will be found to be well adapted for the Harp, by previously tuning the D's flat, then playing it on the open strings in the key of A♭ major, using the Pedals as they are mark'd, wherever accidentals occur." The pedal markings for the harp are omitted in the present edition. Carr slightly modifies Scott's text by inserting exclamations, such as "Oh" and "Ah." Mm. 93 and 106, voice, beat 3, is double-stemmed with one stem beamed with the cue-size notes. Mm. 111–12 and mm. 115–16, beats 1 and 2, LH, the rolled-chord sign is lacking.

[8] Blanche of Devan

M. 25, third word is "made" in Scott.

[9] The Wandering Harper

The author's name is followed by "Esq." M. 10, second word is "no" in Carr. M. 19, RH, beat 1, and m. 21, both hands, beats 1 and 2, cue-size notes are thirty-second-notes—editorially emended by analogy with mm. 1, 2, and 3.

[10] A Weary Lot Is Thine, Sweet Maid

The author's name is followed by "Esq." M. 3, fifth word is "fair" in Scott. M. 5, first word is "pull" and eighth word is "And" in Scott.

[11] Allen-a-Dale

The author's name is followed by "Esq." Verse 4, line 2, last words are "household and home" in Scott. Verse 5, line 2, seventh word is "bade" in Scott.

[12] Thy Smiles Are All Decaying, Love

No variants.

[13] Noah's Dove

No variants.

[14] The Minstrel Knight

M. 11, both hands, beat 1 is a quarter-note. M. 15, LH, beat 1 is an eighth-note. M. 43, LH, beat 2, note 5 is an eighth-note. M. 51, LH, notes 2 and 4 are E-flat.

[15] Sea of Susa

No variants.

[16] Song of the Hebrew Captive. O Sion, O Jerusalem

In Carr's text, "Oh" and "O" are used interchangeably; in the present edition, "O" is adopted throughout to conform to the subtitle. M. 16, voice, beat 2, includes an unnecessary eighth-rest. M. 77, voice, beat 1 is an eighth-note. Differences between Carr's published song (used in the present edition) and his manuscript version are minor and appear mainly in the accompaniment: single notes often replace octaves, the distribution of notes within a chord sometimes varies, pedal indications are lacking, and most tempo, dynamic, and staccato marks are omitted in the manuscript. Other discrepancies in the manuscript are as follows: M. 24, both hands, and m. 25, RH, beats 1 and 2, the rolled-chord sign is lacking. Mm. 35–38, LH, beat 1 is a quarter-note (b-flat, a-natural, a-flat, g, respectively); beat 2 is a quarter-rest. M. 56, LH, six eighth-notes on c'. M. 58, LH, six eighth-notes on a-flat.

[17] An Autumnal Hymn

M. 16, voice, beat 6, eighth-note triplet. M. 42, RH, beat 4 is a quarter-note. M. 43, both hands, beat 4 is a quarter-note.

[18] As Pants the Hart

M. 1, RH, note 6 is e"—editorially emended by analogy with mm. 5, 9, 17, 59, 63, 71, voice, and mm. 24 and 78, RH. M. 20, both hands, beat 3 is a whole-rest. M. 21, voice, cue-size notes are written as full-size notes. M. 24, LH, note 3 is B. M. 58, voice and both hands, beats 3 and 4, half-rest.

[19] A Requiem

The original manuscript is written on two staves. M. 17, RH, beat 3, the lower note of the chord is g, and the natural sign is placed before c'.

[20] Adieu Ye Streams That Sweetly Flow

Unlike most of Carr's songs, both verses are underlaid

in the manuscript; the present edition retains this format. The separate flute and violoncello parts are in D major in the manuscript. The harp-vocal manuscript score, which also includes portions of the flute and violoncello parts in cue-size notes, is in E-flat major, since flat keys were preferred when writing for the harp. M. 17, RH, final chord is a'-flat, c".

[21] *When Nights Were Cold*

The printed versions of the song and the separate flute and violoncello manuscript parts are in A major. The manuscript harp-vocal score, which includes the flute part on the vocal staff during the prelude, interlude, and postlude, is in B-flat major, owing to the preference for flat keys when writing for harp. The critical notes that follow refer to discrepancies between the present edition and the manuscript (primary source) and to major differences between the manuscript and the print. All pitches are given in the key of B-flat major; the original pitch, if in the key of A major, is given in parentheses. M. 11, voice, quarter-note, eighth-note, dotted thirty-second-note, sixty-fourth-note, sixteenth-note in the print. M. 14, voice and flute, note 5, c"-sharp and c'''-sharp (b'-sharp), respectively, in the manuscript; c"-natural (b') is in the print. M. 14, RH, note 8, f' in the manuscript—emended by analogy with g" (f"-sharp) in the flute part, and g' in the vocal part and in the print (f'-sharp) RH. M. 15, voice, beat 1, the turn is from the print. M. 16, harp, beat 2, *sf* is from the print. M. 18, RH, final chord, lower note, b'-natural (a'-sharp) is lacking in the print. Mm. 22 and 24, RH, final four notes are written as two sixteenth-note diads in the print. Mm. 23–26, RH, sixteenth-notes are written as two eighth-note diads in the print. Mm. 23–26, LH, half-note, half-note, half-note, dotted quarter-note on b-flat (a), eighth-rest in the print. M. 30, voice, dotted eighth-note, sixteenth-note, eighth-note, eighth-note; RH, four eighth-notes (or diads) in the print. Verse 2, line 5, seventh word is "look'd" in the print. Verse 3, line 1, third word is "the" in the print.

[22] *Ellen, Arise*

The printed editions do not include flute and violoncello parts; otherwise they are very similar to the manuscript upon which the present edition is based. M. 19, third word is "curs" in both the manuscript and the print. M. 22, violoncello, beat 4, fermata; it does not appear in the other parts. M. 26, LH, beats 1 and 2, whole-rest.

Acknowledgments

The author wishes to thank the Free Library of Philadelphia for making its materials available and for granting permission to publish the facsimiles of Carr's music. Grateful acknowledgment is made to Frederick J. Kent of the Free Library for his valuable assistance, to Rudolph Ellenbogen, Butler Library, Columbia University, and to the staffs of the Library of Congress, New York Public Library, University of Pennsylvania Rare Book Library, Library Company of Philadelphia, and Historical Society of Pennsylvania.

Eve R. Meyer

Notes

1. Carr was a prolific composer of both secular and sacred music. Charles A. Sprenkle, "The Life and Works of Benjamin Carr (1768–1831)" (D.M.A. diss., Peabody Conservatory of Music, 1970), 19, states that approximately 320 compositions by Carr are extant in various libraries and private collections.

2. See the Collection of Trade Cards, no. 88:14, assembled by Ambrose Heal, British Museum, Department of Prints and Drawings. Carr's business card, which is attractively engraved with pictures of musical instruments, reads:

> Benjⁿ / at the Hautboy / in Old Round Court Strand / London / Sells all sorts of Music & / Musical Instru- / ments, Reeds for Hautboys & Bassoons strings / vz. Books of Instructions for all sorts of / Instruments / Music prick'd & Instruments / mended, put in Order & Country Dances Performed / NB All sorts of Stationery &c.

The card is undated, but the date of 1786 has been assigned, possibly by Heal. The present author particularly wishes to thank Donald W. Krummel for locating the above information.

3. Both Robert A. Gerson, *Music in Philadelphia* (Philadelphia, 1940), 51, and Ronnie L. Smith, *The New Grove Dictionary of Music and Musicians*, s.v. "Benjamin Carr," state that Carr also studied with Samuel Wesley, brother of Charles. Samuel Wesley, who was born in 1766, was only two years older than Carr. Although Wesley was a child prodigy, he may not have been considered a suitable teacher for Carr because of his youth. The two men were probably acquainted, but a teacher-pupil relationship is questionable.

4. Doane's *Musical Directory* (1794) lists Carr as "principal tenor, a harpsichordist, and a member of the Academy," according to Philip H. Highfill, Kalman A. Burnim, and Edward A. Langhans, "Benjamin Carr" in *A Biographical Dictionary of Actors, Actresses, Musicians, Dancers, Managers & Other Stage Personnel in London, 1660–1800* (Carbondale, 1975), 3:80. Samuel Arnold was a conductor at the Academy and no doubt was influential in furthering Carr's career as a performer there.

5. In 1792, John Henry, of the Old American Company, and Thomas Wignell, of the New Company, were in London recruiting performers for their theatrical productions, and they may have provided additional inducement. Victor Fell Yellin, "Rayner Taylor," *American Music* 1 (Fall 1983): 49, gives proof that the terminal syllable of Taylor's first name is spelled "er" and not "or," as is commonly found in many modern sources.

6. Thomas Carr (1780–1849), a singer, organist, composer, teacher, and publisher, is best remembered as the arranger and, with his father, the first publisher of "The Star-Spangled Banner."

7. Joseph operated the Philadelphia repository with Benjamin from July of 1793 until the spring of 1794. The Baltimore business was sold by Thomas to George Willig in late 1822, at which time Thomas moved to Philadelphia, where he resumed his musical activities. He is known to have published music there between 1824 and 1827.

8. According to the *American Commercial Advertiser*, Baltimore, 30 October 1819, the Baltimore store also sold technical items, such as telescopes, microscopes, thermometers, and compasses.

9. Proof that Carr received early training as an engraver may be found in Richard J. Wolfe, *Early American Music Engraving and Printing* (Urbana, 1980), xiii, 43. Wolfe mentions an English songsheet of the late 1780s or early 1790s with "B. Carr" given as the engraver. Since Carr pursued so many other activities in America, he probably had little or no time for engraving. Some of the Carr publications state "printed for the composer," and a few give the name of the engraver. The *Musical Journal*, for example, was engraved by I. E. Martin.

10. For additional information on the Carr family as publishers, see Wolfe, *Early American Music Engraving*; Virginia Larkin Redway, "The Carrs, American Music Publishers," *Musical Quarterly* 18 (1932): 150–77; and Helen E. Davis, "The Carrs, A Musical Family," *The Pennsylvania Genealogical Magazine* 24 (1965): 57–68.

11. The most important house was the New Theater on Chestnut Street (later called the Chestnut Street Theater), which opened with a concert of vocal and instrumental music on 2 April 1793. The building was modeled after the Royal Theater in Bath and came to be known as one of the seven wonders of America.

12. For a listing of the professional musicians, see Gerson, *Music in Philadelphia*, 25–26.

13. For the programs of the four concerts presented in the series, see Oscar G. Sonneck, *Early Concert Life in America* (Leipzig, 1907), 95–96. Sonneck also mentions a number of other concerts held in Philadelphia and New York in which Carr was featured as a singer, pianist, or conductor.

14. Ibid., 96. Carr's performance of his own duet, "How Sweet is the Morning," with Miss Broadhurst in Philadelphia, 3 April 1800, is one of the few that can be documented. For the entire program, see ibid., 151.

15. "The Bystander," *Gazette of the United States*, Philadelphia, 25 September 1794.

16. In addition to his performances in churches, Carr initiated outdoor organ concerts in the Pennsylvania Tea Gardens in 1797.

17. Carr received an annual salary of $200 at St. Peter's, according to the Minute Book of the Corporation of the United Episcopal Churches of Christ Church & St. Peter's Church in the City of Philadelphia, 22 April 1816, p. 9, Historical Society of Pennsylvania, Philadelphia. For additional information on wages, the organ, and Carr's predecessors at St. Peter's, see Yellin, "Rayner Taylor," 62–65. St. Augustine's church records were destroyed by fire in 1844.

18. Ronnie L. Smith, "The Church Music of Benjamin Carr (1768–1831)" (D.M.A. diss., Southwestern Baptist Theological Seminary, Texas, 1969), 250, is confident that Carr had the ability to write works of a more demanding nature that would have brought him greater recognition today; as a practical musician, however, Carr needed to provide for the immediate requirements of his choirs. Substantiation of this may be found in Carr's letters to John Rowe Parker regarding Parker's criticism of Carr's collection of sacred music called *The Chorister* (Philadelphia, 1820). Responding to Parker's remark that four-part writing would have been better, Carr commented first on the difficulty of finding "Counter Tenors" for a fourth part and then said that he "generally used 3 parts only as a matter of necessity, not of choice." Carr to Parker, 30 June 1821, John Rowe Parker Letters, Van Pelt Rare Book Library, University of Pennsylvania, Philadelphia.

19. Preface to *Masses, Vespers, Litanies, Hymns, Psalms, Anthems, & Motetts, Composed, Selected and Arranged for the Use of the Catholic Churches in the United States of America* (Baltimore, 1805), RISM: C 1237.

20. Other significant collections in addition to the two mentioned in notes 18 and 19 are *Sacred Harmony, Psalms, Motetts, and*

Sacred Airs (Baltimore and Philadelphia, 1813); *A Collection of Chants and Tunes for the Use of the Episcopal Churches in the City of Philadelphia* (Philadelphia, 1816); and *Collection of Sacred Music, Chants, Anthems, Hymns* (Philadelphia, ca. 1823).

21. The first edition listed 121 initial subscribers.

22. Michael Cross, "Early Music at St. Augustine's Church" in *Historical Sketch of St. Augustine's Church, 1796–1896*, ed. Rev. Francis X. McGowen (Philadelphia, 1896), 41. The author was a descendant of Benjamin Cross, Carr's pupil and friend.

23. *The Euterpeiad, Or Musical Intelligence*, ed. John Rowe Parker (Boston, 1820–23; reprint, New York, 1977).

24. Parker Letters, 31 May 1821.

25. Parker Letters, 4 October 1821.

26. He also wrote unsigned essays about noted London performers under the heading of "Musical Gossip." For a discussion of the influence of Carr's "Musical Reminiscences" on Parker's *Musical Biography*, see John A. Cuthbert," John Rowe Parker and *A Musical Biography*," *American Music* 1 (Summer 1983): 43–46.

27. Parker Letters, 8 September 1820.

28. Parker Letters, 7 December 1821.

29. His portrait, the first to be commissioned by the Society, was painted by J. C. Darley in 1831. Reproductions of the painting, taken from a mezzotint by John Sartain, are available in numerous sources. A few are Highfill, *A Biographical Dictionary*, 3:82; Louis C. Madeira, *Annuals of Music in Philadelphia and History of the Musical Fund Society* (Philadelphia, 1896), frontispiece; Henry Simpson, *The Lives of Eminent Philadelphians* (Philadelphia, 1859), 185; Oscar G. Sonneck, *Early Opera in America* (New York, 1915), 102; Harry Dichter, "Benjamin Carr's 'Musical Journal,' " *Music Journal* 15 (1957): 60; Redway, "The Carrs, American Music Publishers," 154.

30. Carr wrote at length about her studies, her repetoire, and her vocal style in a letter to Parker dated 4 October 1821. For another description of her singing, see "Mrs. French," *The Euterpeiad*, 2:100. Even Mrs. French proved to be a source of frustration for Carr. He was critical of the songs she was currently performing and urged her to rely on "higher sources." She replied that "simple ballads & popular songs were all that was in demand," according to the above-mentioned letter from Carr to Parker.

31. According to a bill made out to Sophia Nathans and receipted by Carr on 29 February 1820, she paid $30 for one quarter's tuition and 5.12^{1/2}$ for assorted sheet music. Elliot Shapiro, "What Price Music?" *The Autograph Collector's Journal* 3 (October 1950): 17.

32. See Julian Mates, *The American Musical Stage before 1800* (New Brunswick, 1962) for an extensive discussion of this work which he makes the focal point of his study of early American opera. Also see *The Musical Works of William Dunlap*, ed. Julian Mates, Scholars' Facsimiles and Reprints, no. 348 (Delmar, New York, 1980) for a facsimile of the text.

33. William Dunlap, *A History of the American Theater* (New York, 1832; reprint, New York, 1963), 288.

34. Carr compiled a catalog of his own compositions on the flyleaf of an untitled eighty-four-page music manuscript book, Carr Notebook No. 159, that is housed in the Hunt-Berol Collection, Butler Library, Columbia University, New York. The notebook contains works for solo voice with piano accompaniment; the only exception is a composition for two flutes. Pages 1–61 are in Carr's hand, pp. 62–65 are blank, and pp. 66–84 are in another hand. The notebook includes the original manuscript for Carr's *Three Ballads from Shakespeare* and songs by Shield, Hook, Arnold, Dibdin, Storace, Handel, and others. The catalog of Carr's compositions cannot be dated precisely, but Carr probably compiled it around 1799. It contains works that were published in 1800, but it does not include compositions that Carr wrote for volume one of the *Musical Journal* (1800) nor does it mention compositions known to have been written after 1800. In addition to theatrical works, the catalog also lists songs, glees, catches, and six piano sonatas. A copy of the catalog is in Redway, "The Carrs, American Music Publishers," 175–76.

35. The instrumental parts were not supplied for the operas imported from England; therefore, the musicians associated with the local opera company were expected to provide suitable orchestral arrangements.

36. This was probably his most successful theatrical work.

37. For a facsimile edition, see *Benjamin Carr's Federal Overture*,

intro. by Irving Lowens (Philadelphia, 1957). A discussion of the work is in Irving Lowens, *Music and Musicians in Early America* (New York, 1964), 89–114.

38. The theatrical scores by Carr and others were lost in the fire that destroyed the Chestnut Street Theater in 1820.

39. For a discussion of the keyboard music, see Byron Adams Wolverton, "Keyboard Music and Musicians in the Colonies and United States of America before 1830" (Ph.D. diss., Indiana University, 1966), and Sprenkle, "The Life and Works of Benjamin Carr." Modern editions of one organ work and three piano compositions are in *Anthology of Early American Keyboard Music, 1787–1830*, ed. J. Bunker Clark, Recent Researches in American Music, vol. 1 (Madison, 1977).

40. William Treat Upton, *Art-Song in America* (New York, 1930), 15.

41. See James Hewitt, *Selected Compositions*, ed. John W. Wagner, Recent Researches in American Music, vol. 7 (Madison, 1980).

42. For a partial list of the published secular music, see Richard J. Wolfe, *Secular Music in America, 1801–1825* (New York, 1964). For other catalogs, see Carroll James Lehman, "Benjamin Carr: His Contribution to Early American Solo Vocal Literature" (D.M.A. diss., University of Iowa, 1975), and Sprenkle, "The Life and Works of Benjamin Carr." The above are only preliminary lists since music is still being discovered. The short catalog in *The New Grove Dictionary*, s.v. "Benjamin Carr," does not clarify which works were composed by Carr and which were arranged or published by him.

43. For a facsimile edition, see *Musical Journal for the Piano Forte*, 2 vols., ed. Benjamin Carr (Wilmington, Del., 1972).

44. Wolfe, *Early American Music Engraving*, 43, calls it "the most important and the most ambitious musical publication issued in America to that time and for a decade or two thereafter."

45. For a facsimile edition, see Benjamin Carr, *Musical Miscellany in Occasional Numbers*, comp. Eve R. Meyer (New York, 1981). Also see Eve R. Meyer, "Benjamin Carr's *Musical Miscellany*," *Notes* 33 (1976): 253–65. Wolfe and other sources give the number of compositions in the *Miscellany* as eighty-five. This author has located an eighty-sixth work, which appears in the above facsimile. Carr did not indicate the final number in the series; thus, one or more additional works may be uncovered at some future date.

46. Carr may have been professionally associated with one or both of these schools. George Schetky is known to have taught at Mrs. Rivardi's Seminary, and Carr's pupil, Mrs. French, attended the school. In a letter to Parker dated 4 October 1821, Carr mentions the high level of musical attainment at the Seminary; he says that concerts of sacred music were presented every Sunday evening and that secular programs were also occasionally given.

47. In Carr's 1793 autograph manuscript of the ballads, only "Tell Me Where Is Fancy Bred" (no. [3]) is written on three staves. Lehman, "Benjamin Carr," 20, is incorrect in stating that Carr's *Musical Journal*, vol. 2 (1800–1801) "initiated in America the printing of songs on three staves, two for the accompaniment and one for the vocal line."

48. For facsimile editions, see Carr's *The History of England*, intro. by Lester S. Levy (Philadelphia, 1954), and *Musical Miscellany*, no. 17.

49. Fortunately, Carr copyrighted a number of his compositions. The copyright date, however, is not always a reliable indication of the composition or even publication date.

50. The Shakespeare ballads were also published in 1794 as Carr's *Four Ballads*, to which "When Nights Were Cold" (no. [21]), on a text by John Edmund Harwood, was added. The three Shakespeare ballads and "Shakespeare's Willow" (no. [4]) have been recorded by Gordon Myers (Parrish Recorded Enterprises, West Trenton, N.J., SPR 1014).

51. Carr was familiar with some of Mozart's operatic works. Carr's "Landing of Columbus," an ode for four-part chorus, for example, is taken from *La clemenza di Tito*; his "History of England" uses "Non più andrai" from *Le nozze di Figaro* as its main theme; and his *Musical Miscellany* includes two arrangements (by other composers) of excerpts from *Die Zauberflöte*. Carr was eager to learn more about Mozart. In a letter to John Rowe Parker dated 8 September 1820, he requests that "the Lives of Haydn and Mozart published in your city" be sent to him. He was referring to the English

translations of the biographies written by Marie Henri Beyle (Stendhal, pseud.) that had been published in London in 1817 and in Boston in 1820.

52. Carr may have been influenced by Thomas Arne's well-known setting of this and other verses from Shakespeare's plays.

53. A brief prelude and postlude have been added to this song in the present edition. To begin with the singer alone and without the key being established would have been highly unlikely at that time. Carr and others suggest that if preludes and postludes have been omitted in the published score, they should be added by the performer. In the preface to *The Caladonian* [sic] *Muse* (ca. 1798), a collection of Scottish music, Carr directs the performer to play the entire air first on the piano and to repeat the last part of the air at the close of every stanza.

54. Other Carr songs in the *Musical Journal* that have not been included in the present edition are volume one, "Poor Mary," "Little Boy Blew," "Ah! How Hapless Is the Maiden," "The Widow"; volume two, "Zephyrs of the Vernal Morn," "A Negro Song," "The Orphan Boy," "The Poor Flower Girl"; volume three, "Erin Go Bragh," "A Little Ballad"; volume four, "The Morning Dew," "Claudine," "Rondeau Chasse" (with George Schetky); volume five, "The Willows Wave over His Tomb."

55. For sources that contain reproductions of this song, see H. Wiley Hitchcock, *American Music before 1865 in Print and on Records*, Institute for Studies in American Music Monographs, no. 6 (New York, 1976), 12, 37, 58, 60, 62, 64.

56. Ballads not included in the present anthology are "Mary," "Alice Brand," and "Coronach." The latter was "principally adapted to an ancient Gaelic Air." The six songs are recorded in *The Flowering of Vocal Music in America*, vol. 2 (New World Records NW 231).

57. This poem was also set to music by the English composer Thomas Attwood in the same year.

58. Carr wrote several bravura arias, usually with one or more professional singers in mind. One such example is "Ah! How Hapless Is the Maiden," published in vol. 1 of the *Musical Journal* (1800). The work was a concert hall favorite and was frequently performed by Miss Broadhurst, Mrs. Oldmixon, and Mrs. Hodgkinson. The brilliant roulades in the aria's allegro section sound stiff and unmusical. Carr was much more successful in later works, such as "Hymn to the Virgin," when he shortened and simplified the florid passages.

59. Upton, *Art-Song in America*, 22.

60. Ibid.

61. H. Wiley Hitchcock, *Music in the United States* (Englewood Cliffs, N.J., 1969), 30.

62. "Brignal Banks," which has a trio refrain, is the only one of the four *Rokeby* ballads that is not included in the present anthology. As no. 22 in the *Musical Miscellany* series, Carr added another *Rokeby* setting, the duet "The Tear Down Childhood's Cheek That Flows." Other songs by Carr in the *Musical Miscellany* that are not in the present edition are "Yes, Henry, Yes," "The History of England," "Moonlight at Sea," "In Thy Soft Bewitching Glances," "Cupid Awaken'd," and "Walk Fast, My Dearest Lad."

63. Songs from Carr's *Canzonetts* not included in the present anthology are "The Gondolier," "The Firefly," and "Thou Faithful Guardian."

64. Headings such as *ballad* or *canzonet* were employed in a rather flexible manner in the early nineteenth century. An examination of the music indicates that restrictive definitions as to style, poetic content, or even form cannot be applied. *Ballad*, for example, appeared as the heading for both narrative and non-narrative songs, and *canzonet* could be used for strophic as well as non-strophic compositions. Nicholas Temperley, *English Songs 1800–1860*, Musica Britannica, no. 43 (London, 1979), xvii, says that *canzonet* had been used in late eighteenth-century England as "the name for a somewhat more serious type of song, generally (but not always) a continuous rather than a strophic composition."

65. Songs from Carr's *Sacred Airs* not included in the present anthology are "Wandering Pilgrims" ("arranged from Kozeluch"), "The Vesper Star," "What Is Prayer?" and "The Hour of Prayer." Carr added the *Sacred Airs* in the appendix to the 1830 edition of *Masses, Vespers, Litanies* (see note 19).

66. In his catalog of Carr's works, Sprenkle, "The Life and

Works of Benjamin Carr," lists "From Psalm 137" as a separate composition. It is, however, the manuscript version of "Song of the Hebrew Captive."

67. The similarity was noted in Lehman, "Benjamin Carr," 82.

68. Grace D. Yerbury, *Song in America from Early Times to about 1850* (Metuchen, N.J., 1971), 75–76.

69. Parker, *Euterpeiad* 1 (16 September 1820): 99.

70. Parker, "Mrs. French," *Euterpeiad* 2 (15 September 1821): 100.

71. Benjamin Carr, *Analytical Instructor for the Pianoforte,* Op. 15 (Philadelphia, 1826), 55.

72. Benjamin Carr, *Lessons and Exercises in Vocal Music,* Op. 8 (Philadelphia, ca. 1811), RISM: C 1239. The manual is undated, but since Carr published his Op. 7 (*Lady of the Lake* ballads) in 1810 and his Op. 9 (*Six Progressive Sonatinas*) in about 1812, 1811 would be the logical approximate date for the *Lessons.*

73. *Lessons and Exercises,* 37.

74. Ibid., 48.

75. Ibid., 30.

76. Ibid., 30–31.

77. Ibid., 33.

78. Ibid., 29.

79. Ibid., 42.

80. Ibid., 40.

81. *New Serial Titles* (Library of Congress, Washington, D.C., 1983).

Plate I. Benjamin Carr, "Ellen, Arise," B. Carr, Philadelphia, ca. 1798, page one.
(Courtesy of the Free Library of Philadelphia)

Plate II. Benjamin Carr, "Ellen, Arise," *Armonia domestica* (autograph manuscript), page twelve. (Courtesy of the Free Library of Philadelphia)

[1] When Icicles Hang by the Wall

[William] Shakespeare

When blood be nipt and ways be foul, Then night-ly sings the star-ing owl, "Tu-

- whit, Tu- woo, Tu- woo!"— A mer-ry, mer-ry note, While greas-y

Joan doth keel the pot, While greas-y Joan doth keel the pot.

When all aloud the wind doth blow
And coughing drowns the parson's saw
And birds sit brooding in the snow
And Marian's nose looks red and raw,
When roasted crabs hiss in the bowl,
Then nightly sings the staring owl,
"Tu-whit, Tu-woo, Tu-woo!"
A merry, merry note,
While greasy Joan doth keel the pot,
While greasy Joan doth keel the pot.

4

[2] Take, Oh, Take Those Lips Away

[William] Shakespeare

Take, Oh, take those lips a-way, That so sweet- ly were for-

- sworn;_ And those eyes, at_ break_of_ day, Lights_that do_ mis- lead the morn;_

Lights _____ that_ do _____ mis- lead the morn;

[attributed to John Fletcher]

Hide, Oh! hide those hills of snow,
Which thy frozen bosom bears,
On whose tops the pinks that grow;
Are of those that April wears;
[Are of those that April wears;]
But my poor heart first set free,
Bound in icy chains by thee.
[But my poor heart first set free, first set free,
Bound in icy chains by thee.]

6

[3] Tell Me Where Is Fancy Bred

[William] Shakespeare

Tell me where is fan- cy bred, Or in the heart or in the head? How be- got, how nour-ish'd?

How be- got, how nour-ish'd? Re- ply, re- ply. So it en- gen- der'd

in the eyes, With gaz- ing fed; and fan- cy dies In the cra- dle where it lies. Let us all ring fan- cy's knell; I'll be- gin it, Ding, dong, bell. Ding, dong, bell. Ding, ding, ding, ding, ding, ding, dong, bell. Ding, ding, ding, ding, ding, ding, dong, bell.

8

[4] Shakespeare's Willow

[William Shakespeare]

O   the green wil-low,   shall   be my gar- land.

2. She sigh'd in her singing—sigh'd and after each moan—
        O willow, willow, willow;
   I am dead to all pleasure my true love is gone—
        O willow, willow, willow, willow,
   Sing O the green willow, O the green willow,
        O the green willow, shall be my garland.

3. The willow now bids me—bids me despair and to die—
        O willow, willow, willow;
   So hang it friends o'er me in grave where I lie—
        O willow, willow, willow, willow,
   Sing O the green willow, O the green willow,
        O the green willow, shall be my garland.

[5] Why, Huntress, Why

[William Dunlap]

friends. Why, hunt- ress, why wilt thou thy life ex- pose, So

val- - ued by thy friends.

If thou shouldst fall, the death of all our

foes, If thou shouldst fall, the death of all our foes Can nev- er make a- mends.

Then, hunt-ress, why wilt thou thy life ex- pose?

2. Ah! think what pangs thy father still must feel,
   What pangs must Arnold know,
   [What pangs must Arnold know,
   What pangs must Arnold know,
   Ah! think what pangs thy father still must feel,
   What pangs must Arnold know,]
   When thou'rt expos'd unto the biting steel,
   [When thou'rt expos'd unto the biting steel,]
   Shall rush amid the foe.
   Then, huntress, why wilt thou thy life expose?

[6] Soldier, Rest!

[Sir Walter Scott]

Sol- dier, rest! thy war- fare o'er, Sleep ___ the sleep ___ that knows ___ no break- ing;

Dream of bat- tled fields no more, Days ___ of dan- ger, nights ___ of wak- ing.

In our isle's en- chant- ed hall, Hands ___ un- seen ___ thy couch ___ is strew- ing,

14

2. No rude sound shall reach thine ear,
      Armour's clang or war-steed champing,
   Trump nor pibroch summon here
      Mustering clan or squadron tramping.
   Yet the lark's shrill fife may come
      At the daybreak from the fallow,
   And the bittern sound his drum,
      Booming from the sedgy shallow.
   Ruder sounds shall none be near,
   Guards nor warders challenge here,
   Here's no war-steed's neigh and champing,
   Shouting clans or squadrons stamping.

3. Huntsman, rest! thy chase is done;
      While our slumbrous spells assail ye,
   Dream not, with the rising sun,
      Bugles here shall sound reveille.
   Sleep! the deer is in his den;
   Sleep! thy hounds are by thee lying:
   Sleep! nor dream in yonder glen
      How thy gallant steed lay dying.
   Huntsman, rest! thy chase is done;
   Think not of the rising sun,
   For at dawning to assail ye
   Here no bugles sound reveille.

[7] Hymn to the Virgin
Ave Maria

[Sir Walter Scott]

de-mons__ of __ the __ earth and air, From this their wont-ed haunt ex-il'd, Shall flee be-fore thy pres-ence fair,

thy pres-ence fair. _____ We bow us __ to __ our lot __ of _____ care, ___ Be-

- neath thy __ guid-ance re-con-cil'd: _ Maid-en! Maid-en! Hear _____

___ for a maid __ a maid-en's __ pray'r, Moth-er, Moth-er, And _____

A- ve Ma- ri-

- a,

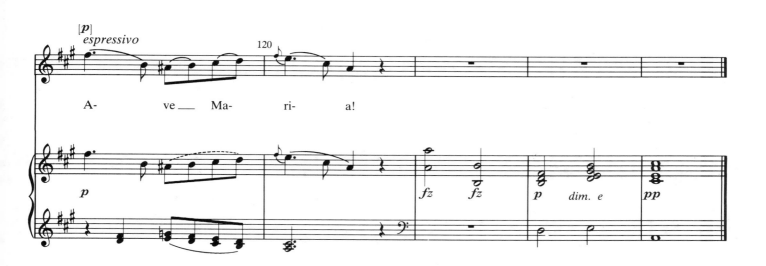

A- ve Ma- ri- a!

[8] Blanche of Devan

[Sir Walter Scott]

Moderato e agitato

They bid me sleep, they bid me pray, They say my brain is warp'd and

wrung— I can-not sleep on High-land brae, I can-not pray in High-land tongue. But were I

now where Al-lan glides, Or heard my na- tive De- van's tides, So sweet- ly — wou'd I

[dolce e piu lento]

dolce e piu lento

rest, __ and __ pray That Heav'n would __ close __ my __ win- try __ day! That Heav'n would

close my win- try day! 'Twas thus my hair they bade me braid, They bade me

to the church re- pair; It was my brid- al morn, they said, And my true love wou'd meet me

there. But woe be- tide the cru- el guile That drown'd in blood the morn-ing smile! And

28

woe— be- tide the fair- y— dream! I on- ly— wak'd_to— sob— and—

scream. I on- ly wak'd to sob and scream. I on- ly wak'd to sob and scream.

[9] The Wandering Harper

[Sir] Walter Scott

Sum- mer _ eve is gone and _ past,

Sum- mer _ dew is fall- ing fast;

2. Bid not me, in battle-field,
   Buckler lift or broadsword wield!
   All my strength and all my art
   Is to touch the gentle heart
   With the wizard notes that ring, (the notes that ring)
   From the peaceful minstrel-string, (the minstrel-string.)

3. I have song of war for knight,
   Lay of love for lady bright,
   Fairy tale to lull the heir,
   Goblin grim the maids to scare.
   Dark the night and long till day, (and long till day,)
   Do not bid me farther stray, (not farther stray!)

4. Rokeby's lords of martial fame,
   I can count them name by name;
   Legends of their line there be,
   Known to few but known to me;
   If you honour Rokeby's kin, (Rokeby's kin,)
   Take the wand'ring harper in, (O take him in!)

5. Rokeby's lords had fair regard
   For the harp and for the bard;
   Baron's race throve never well
   Where the curse of minstrel fell.
   If you love that noble kin, (that noble kin,)
   Take the weary harper in, (O take him in!)

[10] A Weary Lot Is Thine, Sweet Maid

[Sir] Walter Scott

A wea-ry lot is thine, sweet maid, A wea-ry lot is thine! To pluck the thorn thy brow to braid, To press the rue for wine! A light-some eye, a sol-dier's mien, A feath-er of the blue, A dou-blet of the Lin-coln green, No more of me you knew, My love! No more of me you knew.

This morn is mer-ry June, I trow, The rose is bud- ing fain; But

she shall bloom in win- ter snow Ere we two meet a- gain. He turn'd his charg- er as he spake Up-

-on the riv- er shore, He gave his bri- dle-reins a _____ shake, Said, "A-

- dieu for ev-er-more, My love! And a- dieu for ev- er- more."

34

[11] Allen-a-Dale

[Sir] Walter Scott

Allegro moderato

Al- len- a- Dale,

Al- len- a- Dale, Al- len- a- Dale has no fag- got for burn- ing,

Al- len- a- Dale has no fur- row for turn- ing, Al- len- a- Dale has no

2. [Allen-a-Dale, Allen-a-Dale,]
   The Baron of Ravensworth prances in pride,
   And he views his domains upon Arkindale side.
   The mere for his net and the land for his game,
   The chase for the wild and the park for the tame;
   Yet the fish of the lake and the deer of the vale
   Are less free to Lord Dacre than Allen-a-Dale!
   [Allen-a-Dale, Allen-a-Dale,
   And tell me the craft of bold Allen-a-Dale.]

3. [Allen-a-Dale, Allen-a-Dale,]
   Allen-a-Dale was ne'er belted a knight,
   Though his spur be as sharp and his blade be as bright;
   Allen-a-Dale is no baron or lord,
   Yet twenty tall yeomen will draw at his word;
   And the best of our nobles his bonnet will vail,
   Who at Rere-cross on Stanmore meets Allen-a-Dale!
   [Allen-a-Dale, Allen-a-Dale,]
   And tell me the craft of bold Allen-a-Dale.]

4. [Allen-a-Dale, Allen-a-Dale,]
   Allen-a-Dale to his wooing is come;
   The mother, she asked of his house and his home;
   "Though the castle of Richmond stand fair on the hill,
   My hall," quoth bold Allen, "shows gallanter still;
   'Tis the blue vault of heaven, with its crescent so pale
   And with all its bright spangles!" said Allen-a-Dale.
   [Allen-a-Dale, Allen-a-Dale,
   And tell me the craft of bold Allen-a-Dale.]

5. [Allen-a-Dale, Allen-a-Dale,]
   The father was steel and the mother was stone;
   They lifted the latch and they bid him be gone;
   But loud on the morrow their wail and their cry;
   He had laughed on the lass with his bonny black eye,
   And she fled to the forest to hear a love-tale
   And the youth it was told by was Allen-a-Dale!
   [Allen-a-Dale, Allen-a-Dale,
   And tell me the craft of bold Allen-a-Dale.]

[12] Thy Smiles Are All Decaying, Love

[James Gates] Percival

-cay- ing, Love, The smile that once was play- ing, Love,

The smile that once was play- ing, Love, So pure and bright, It

seem'd but light, From days clear foun- tain stray- ing, Love.

2. That lip will shed its sweetness, Love,
   Thy form will lose its fleetness, Love,
   [Thy form will lose its fleetness, Love,]
      Arrayed no more,
      As when it wore
  The snowy veil of neatness, Love.

3. The rose of youth is blowing, Love,
   The tide of health is flowing, Love,
   [The tide of health is flowing, Love,]
      Then let it be,
      Entwin'd to thee
  As elms and vines are growing, Love.

4. A chain of flow'rs has twin'd us, Love,
   And blest the hours shall find us, Love,
   [And blest the hours shall find us, Love,]
      Then from the heart
      No more shall part,
  Till age and death unbind us, Love.

[13] Noah's Dove

soon my dis- ap-point- ed heart, But soon my dis- ap-point- ed heart, Like

No- ah's Dove,_ Like No- ah's_ Dove,_ Like No- ah's Dove, Like No-ah's Dove re-turn'd_a-

piu lento

[piu lento]

- gain.

pp

2. Another resting place it sought,
   Entic'd by Emma's sprightly mien,
   [Another resting place it sought,
   Entic'd by Emma's sprightly mien,]
   But like that dove return'd and brought,
   [But like that dove return'd and brought,]
   Only a token, only a token where it had been,
   A token where it had been.

3. But soon as Julia charm'd my sight,
   With beauty's smiles and virtue's lore,
   [But soon as Julia charm'd my sight,
   With beauty's smiles and virtue's lore,]
   Like that same bird it took its flight,
   [Like that same bird it took its flight,]
   And finding rest return'd no more, return'd no more,
   And finding rest return'd no more.

[14] The Minstrel Knight

Allegro moderato

A wan- d'ring min- strel wea- ry___ came To a cas- tle

at an ev'- ning hour, Where man-y a knight and love- ly___ dame Were met to

strung.

A maid with- in this cas- tle ___ dwelt, More fair than

poco lento   **tempo**

an-y that grac'd the hall; Tho' man-y a knight to her ___ had ___ knelt, She lov'd the

min- strel best of all.   In ___ bard's dis- guise to

her — he — sung, But his name was of an-cient no- ble pride, And his

harp so sweet- ly to love — was — strung, That she now is his bloom- ing bride, That she

now is his bloom- ing — bride; So sweet- ly, sweet- ly, sweet- ly — to —

love his harp — was — strung.

44

[15] Sea of Susa

2. 'Twas from my window first I spied
My love, as past he chanc'd to ride:
['Twas from my window first I spied
My love, as past he chanc'd to ride:]
In gayest colours was he dress'd
With crimson robe and yellow vest.
Oh! tell me Sea of Susa tell
If on your banks my love does dwell.

3. Before my friends, dear youth! I seem
Thy worth but little to esteem;
[Before my friends, dear youth! I seem
Thy worth but little to esteem;]
But in my heart could'st thou but see
I languish and I die, for thee.
Oh! tell me Sea of Susa tell
If on your banks my love does dwell.

[16] Song of the Hebrew Captive
O Sion, O Jerusalem

[Psalm 137]

hand for-get to strike the sound-ing lyre, the sound-ing lyre, _____

the sound- -ing lyre,

the sound-

[17] An Autumnal Hymn

David Paul Brown, Esq.

[18] As Pants the Hart

Psalm 42

58

soul's cast down, O Lord, but think of thee and Si- on _

still, From Jor- dan's bank, from Her- mon's height and _ Mi-zar's hum- bler, _

Major tempo [primo]

hum- bler hill. But when _ thy _ pres- ence, Lord _ of _ life, has once dis-pell'd this

[tempo primo]

storm, To thee _ I'll _ mid- night an- thems _ sing and all _____ my vows per-

- form. _____ Then I'll ad-vance with songs of praise my sol- emn, sol- emn

vows to pay _____ And lead __ the __ joy- ful sa- cred __ throng to

keep the fes- tal day, _____ to keep _____ the fes- tal

day. _____

[19] A Requiem

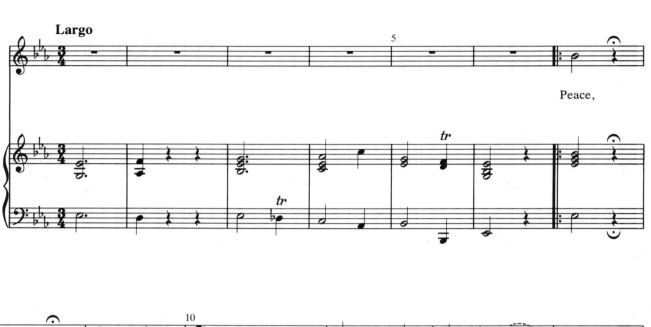

Peace,

peace, peace to thy gen- tle shade, and end- less rest, __ Thy __ er- rors

par- don'd and thy vir- tues blest. Sleep

sweet- ly___ sleep be-neath this dew- y sod,___ 'Till an- gels wake thee,

wake thee, to meet thy God, to___ meet,_ to meet thy God.

[20] Adieu Ye Streams That Sweetly Flow

66

gales   that soft- ly ___ blow,   soft- ly blow,   soft- ly ___
tear,   nor heave ___ one ___ sigh,   one ___ sigh,   drop ___ one ___

soft- ly, soft- ly blow.
tear, _____ nor heave   ly one sigh.

Ye   plains ___ by   bloom- ing
But   forc'd ___ from   Del- ia's

birds   that war- ble,   that war- ble, war- ble   in   the

cheer   my droop-ing,   my droop- ing, droop- ing, droop-   ing

shade.

heart.

[21] When Nights Were Cold

[John Edmund] Harwood

mile My lov- er trav- ell'd to __ be- hold _____ me.

[sf]

His toil re- paid to see __ me __ smile And sweet- ly

in his arms __ en- fold __ me. And __ thro' the night we'd

sit and chat; A- las! there was no harm in that. And thro' the night we'd

sit and chat; A- las! there was no harm in that, A- las! there was no

harm in that.

2. How sweet his words when e'er he spoke,
   But oh! when he his passion broke,
   Upon his lips the falt'ring tale
   More grace received from his confusion,
   And now by turns his cheek grew pale,
   Or crimson'd o'er with mild suffusion.
   Our beating hearts went pit-a-pat;
   Alas! there was no harm in that,
   [Our beating hearts went pit-a-pat;
   Alas! there was no harm in that,
   Alas! there was no harm in that.]

3. Another now that bliss must prove,
   Tho' we so oft have sworn to love,
   O cruelty my heart will break;
   I'll hie me to some shade forsaken,
   And only of my love I'll speak,
   And prove my faith and truth unshaken.
   I'll wander where we oft have sat;
   Sure there will be no harm in that,
   [I'll wander where we oft have sat;
   Sure there will be no harm in that,
   Sure there will be no harm in that.]

[22] Ellen, Arise

[John Edmund] Harwood

See from yon cot- tage __ win- dow plays The friend- ly ta- per's __ trem- bling light, To

guide me on the path- way strays And cheers the gloom of

com- ing night, And cheers the gloom of com- ing night,

And cheers the gloom of com- ing night.

The trust- y course my___ steps dis- cov- er;___

El- len, a-rise, it is thy faith- ful___ lov- er, El- len, a- rise,___

El- len, a- rise,___ El- len, a- rise, a- rise, it is thy faith- ful___

lov- er, El-len, a- rise, it is thy__ faith- ful __ lov- er.

2. Long had she mark'd the tedious hour,
   The clicking dial's tardy sound,
   Fancy'd full oft the pelting show'r
   Beat rudely, beat upon the ground;
   [Beat rudely, beat upon the ground;
   Beat rudely, beat upon the ground;]
   But love dispers'd the storm above her,
   Hark, Ellen, hark, it is thy faithful lover,
   Hark, Ellen, hark, hark, Ellen, hark,
   Hark, Ellen, hark, it is thy faithful lover,
   Hark, Ellen, hark, it is thy faithful lover.

3. The threshold meets his footsteps light,
   The kiss repays his labor done;
   Now friendly is the gloom of night,
   For lovers bless the absent sun,
   [For lovers bless the absent sun,
   For lovers bless the absent sun.]
   Now, Ellen, now, thou may'st discover
   It is indeed thy own, thy faithful lover,
   It is indeed, it is indeed,
   It is indeed thy own, thy faithful lover,
   It is indeed thy own, thy faithful lover.

APPENDIX

The Vi'let Nurs'd in Woodland Wild

From *Lessons and Exercises in Vocal Music,* Op. 8

See p. 85 for Carr's Key to Symbols

self _____ in- spires _____ the strain.

Their__ melt- ing mu- sic

fails   to please, Their__ melt- ing mu- sic   fails   to please,   Harsh and un-tune-ful

are   their   lays, __ When Phil- o- mel __ a-   wakes __ the ____ plain,   a-

- wakes _ the _ plain, a- wakes, _____ a- wakes _____ the plain, The _

feath- er'd _ tribes who _ in their _ groves, With _ trills mel- lif- luous _ woo their _ loves,

Harsh and un-tune- ful are their lays, Harsh and un-tune- ful are their lays, When

Phil- o- mel a- wakes _ the _ plain, a- wakes _ the _ plain, a- wakes, _____ a- wakes, _____

a- wakes, _____ a-

- wakes, _____ a- wakes _____ the plain, _____ a-

- wakes the plain.

Key to Symbols

⌐ This mark is where the breath should be taken.

∧ This [is] where Emphasis is to be laid.

1. Appoggiatura

2. Appoggiatura

3. Unprepared inverted turn

4. Appoggiatura

5. Shake

6. Appoggiatura

7. Transient shake

8. Prepared turn

9. Appoggiatura

10. Shake and grace afterwards

11. Short appoggiatura

12. Unprepared inverted turn

13. Unprepared inverted turn

14. Prepared turn

15. Prepared inverted turn

16. The crescendo—swell the voice loud, louder.

17. Shake with a conclusive grace

[18. Appoggiatura]

19. Prepared turns

20. Prepared turns [see no. 19]

21. Portamento—swell the voice to loud then diminish the tone.

22. Plain shake without a concluding grace

23. Appoggiatura

24. Appoggiatura

25. Shake and grace

26. Unprepared inverted turn

27. Unprepared inverted turn [see no. 26]

28. Portamento—gradually swell the voice to loud then diminish the tone.

29. A succession of prepared turns

30. Plain shake without a conclusive grace

31. The syllable is here not completed [a-a-a], merely to show that in staccato passages on notes in Alt or high notes to words concluding with consonants it is allowable to finish with the Vowel omitting the consonants at the end. The above are given merely as an example, as it is to be observed that staccato notes or the omittance of a conclusive vowel usually occur upon notes higher in the scale than those—but as the wish was to make this song useful, care has been [taken] not to extend its compass beyond the general run of voices.

32. Shake and turn